**BÜRO
DESTI**
DIE GESTAL
VERLAG

CW00959117

Dedicated to our parents

Büro Destruct Berne Capital
Wasserwerkgasse 7
CH-3011 Bern
Switzerland

Fax: +41 (0)31 312 63 07
bd@bermuda.ch
www.burodestruct.net
www.typedifferent.com
www.loslogos.org
www.burodiscount.net

ISBN 3-89955-002-1

Edited by Robert Klanten
Published by Die Gestalten
Verlag, Berlin

Printed by Medialis
Offsetdruck GmbH, Berlin
Made in Europe

Bibliographic information
published by Die Deutsche
Bibliothek
Die Deutsche Bibliothek
lists this publication in the
Deutsche Nationalbibliografie;
detailed bibliographic data
is available in the Internet at
http://dnb.ddb.de.

© dgv- Die Gestalten Verlag,
Berlin 2003

Typed with
55 Helvetica Neue Roman 7Pt

Produced with Adobe
InDesign 2.0.2
Illustrator 10.0.3
Photoshop 7.0.1
Lightwave 7.5
on Macintosh OSX 10.2.5

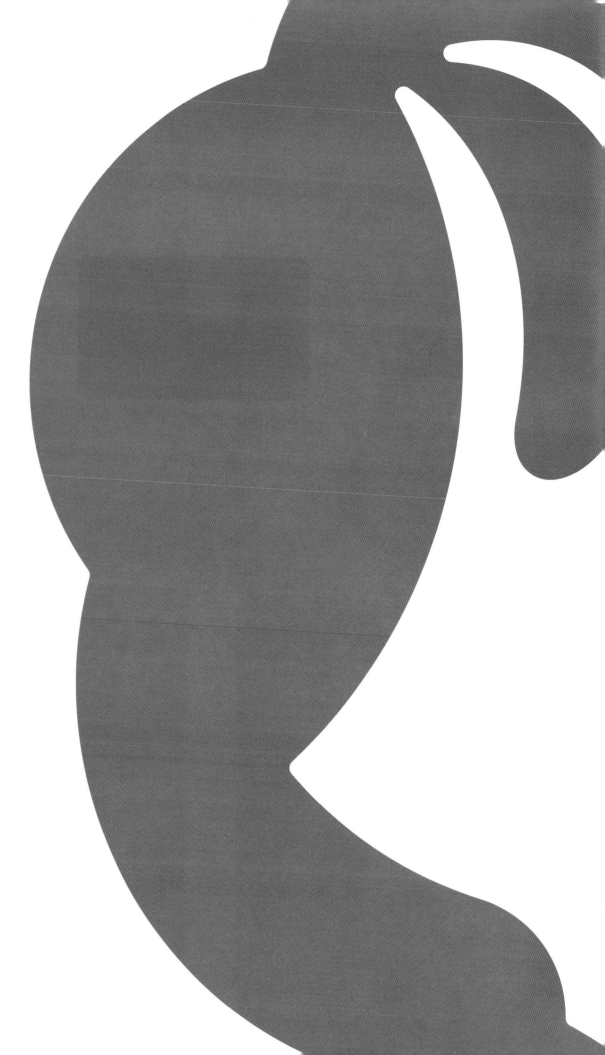

BÜRO
DESTRUCT II

HGB Fideljus Berger

Lopetz, Claudio & Michael Gianfreda

MB & Jürg Brunner

H1 & Wendelin Reber

Moritz & Sabine Adler

Heiwid & Urs Widmer

Beim Barte des Propheten

Das Land, aus dem wir kommen, ist klein und die Stadt, in der wir leben, ist ebenfalls dementsprechend klein. Schweizer Produkten haftet nach wie vor, auch nach dem Sinkflug unserer nationalen Fluggesellschaft Swissair, das Image für präzises, praktisches und zuverlässiges Handwerk an. Geschätzte Merkmale unseres Volkes sind angeblich: Ordentlichkeit, Gründlichkeit und Sauberkeit. Als eines der wenigen Länder Europas gehört die Schweiz immer noch nicht der Europäischen Union (EU) an. Es befindet sich so gesehen eingekesselt zwischen Bergen in einer Art Käseglocke mit Schokoladenüberzug. Toblerone, die weltbekannte Schokolade in Form einer Bergkette, stammt aus unserer Heimatstadt Bern. Sie ist unterdessen im Besitz des Veni-vidi-vici-Weltkonzerns Philip Morris – schade. Dafür haben wir jetzt ein Tobleronemuseum bekommen, auch nicht schlecht, Kultur hat schließlich ihren Preis. Die Schweiz ist also ein friedliches und stilles Land. Ein Land auch, das auf den ersten Blick sicher keinen Nährboden für kreative Ausbrüche oder dergleichen bietet. Und genau hier verbirgt sich vielleicht das Geheimnis der berühmten Schweizer Qualität und möglicherweise einer der Gründe für die hohe Reputation der Schweizer Grafik: Es ist Zeit und Ruhe vorhanden, die einem die Möglichkeit gibt, um exakt und fleissig – wie eine Biene – arbeiten zu können.

Keine Frage, wir hatten auch Glück und Glück ist schön. Von unserer Familie haben wir immer viel Liebe gekriegt. Liebe ist keine Selbstverständlichkeit und Freundschaft bedeutet Glück. Wenn es darum geht, vorne mit dabei zu sein, dann sind die Freundschaft und die Liebe ganz vorne mit dabei. Liebe bringen wir auch unserer Arbeit, die sich manchmal wie ein wildes Kind aufführt, entgegen.

Auch die Kunst bedeutet uns viel. Wir alle wissen nicht genau, was sie bedeutet, aber wir alle wissen, dass sie uns was bedeutet. In den letzten Jahren haben wir kapiert: Wenn wir von Kunst sprechen, dann reden wir eigentlich mehr von Leben, von einem bestimmten Lebensstil, von einer ganz bestimmten Haltung. Und wenn wir von dieser Haltung sprechen, dann reden wir von dem, was wir «Hundert Prozent Groove» nennen und stehen damit vieleicht 15 Meter näher bei Popbands wie Kraftwerk, KLF oder den Sex Pistols, als bei unseren Vorbildern wie Marcel Duchamp, Claes Oldenburg oder Jacques Tati. Statt über Kunst- und Kulturmechanismen zu philosophieren, rauchen wir heute lieber zusammen eine Pfeife drauf. Gymnastics interessiert uns mehr. Der Spagat und der Acrobat auf der Schnittstelle zwischen Kunst, Grafikdesign und Werbung. Doch wir selbst wissen manchmal nicht wirklich, was Büro Destruct ist und vielleicht haben gerade andere Menschen eine viel realistischere Vorstellung davon. Sicher ist – Büro Destruct ist ein unheimliches Gefühl.

In unserer Ausbildung zum Grafiker, damals natürlich noch ohne Computer und dazugehörende Software, also noch nach alter Schule mit Touche, Pinsel, Reissfeder und Lineal, war beispielsweise das Fachgebiet Schriftenmalen eine echte Plage. Erst durch die Arbeit mit dem Computer wurde unser Freudenfeuer für die Erstellung von Schriften wirklich entfacht. Die Möglichkeit, auf einer Tastatur die selbstkreierten Schriften tippen und uneingeschränkt nutzen zu können, ist für uns ein unglaublich großer Motivationsfaktor. Das hat nichts (oder nur wenig) mit Faulheit, mit Müßiggang zu tun, denn der Glaube, dass eine Maschine die Freiheit einschränkt, ist unserer Meinung nach ein Irrtum. Wir glauben, dass man freier ist, wenn man eine Maschine bedient, nicht nur, weil man schneller ist, sondern weil eine Maschine besser als Reissfeder und Lineal das Überschreiten von Regeln gestattet. Das Überschreiten von Regeln macht die Regel erst richtig augenfällig.

Wie sich der Filmemacher Jean-Luc Godard als Organisator von Bildern und Tönen bezeichnet, so ähnlich sehen wir uns als Organisator von Bildern und Schriftzeichen. Malen und Zeichnen ist für uns eine Art Suche. Eine Suche, wie es wahrscheinlich bei jeder kreativen Tätigkeit eine Voraussetzung ist. Es ist eine Suche, die uns von einem Strich oder einer Form zum nächsten Strich und zur nächsten Form führt. Eins zieht das andere nach sich. Eine wunderschöne Tätigkeit, um ganz nah bei sich selbst und seinen Nächsten zu sein. Für uns einer der «Holy Moments» die wir suchen. Man sollte immer nur das nächstliegende vor Augen haben und nicht zu weit vorausdenken. Wie der Lernprozess eines Kindes viel Geduld erfordert, erfordert auch das Malen und Zeichnen viel Geduld. Ungeduld ist wie Gift für die Kreativität.
Mit diebischer Freude sollte man sich erdreisten, sich wie ein Kind aufzuführen. Gute Maler, die es verstehen, mit Farben umzugehen, sind – Kinder. Sie drücken aus, was sie fühlen. Das Schöne an der Welt ist, dass sie verändert werden kann! Kurzum: leben. Arthur Rimbaud sagte: «Kein Mensch hat jemals etwas erschaffen.» Der Künstler kann nichts erschaffen. Er kann die Dinge nur neu ordnen und organisieren.
Wir beanspruchen eine Menge Narrenfreiheit. Eine Narrenfreiheit, die mehr mit unbändigem Wissensdrang als mit elitärer Borniertheit zu tun hat. Auch wenn das Kind Büro Destruct unterdessen Bart trägt und vielleicht ein wenig älter und weiser geworden ist, will es immer noch forschen, weiterlernen und mitspielen. Spielen stand schon immer weit oben auf der Prioritätenliste von Büro Destruct und deshalb würden wir keine Sekunde zögern, um das Statement «Karrieristen sind nicht cool» der britischen Popband Pet Shop Boys zu unterschreiben. In unserer Arbeit geht es letztlich um die Individualität zu Gunsten einer kollektiven Identität. Keine Carte Blanche, sondern eine Carte Orange!

Gerade wenn wir von unserer Arbeit sprechen, dann sehen wir uns besonders tief verbunden mit Waldmenschen und Wiesengeister. Von ganz weit weg kommen die Lichter und die Geräusche: Wie ein Trommelwirbel im Zweivierteltakt oder ein bisschen mehr. Wie eine

By the Prophet's Beard

The country we are from is small and the city we live in is accordingly small also. Even after the descent of our national airline, Swiss products are still associated with the image of precise, practical and reliable craft. Apparently the appreciated virtues of our people are orderliness, thoroughness and cleanliness. Switzerland is one of the few European countries that still doesn't belong to the European Union (EU). You can look at Switzerland as a country boxed in between mountains, in a cheese bell coated with chocolate. Toblerone, the famous chocolate shaped after a chain of mountains and appreciated throughout the world, is made in Bern, our hometown. It's a pity that Toblerone now belongs to the veni-vidi-vici Philip Morris Corporation. Although we did get a Toblerone museum as consolation, that's also not bad – culture has its price after all. So Switzerland is a peaceful and quiet country. A country also, which at first sight offers no fertile ground for creative eruptions. This may be exactly where the secret of Swiss quality lies and possibly one of the reasons for the high esteem of Swiss graphic design. There is time and tranquility that gives us the chance to work precisely and assiduously – like the bees.

Beyond doubt, we have been lucky – and luck is a wonderful thing. Our families always gave us a lot of love. You can't take love for granted and friendship is bliss. You cannot be at the top without love and friendship. We also show love for our work – the work that sometimes acts like a wild child.

Art means a lot to us. None of us knows exactly what it means, but we know it means something. In the last few years we have realised that, by mentioning art, we actually speak of life as such, of a certain lifestyle, of a specific attitude. Mentioning this attitude, we mean what we call «Hundred Percent Groove» and thereby stand maybe fifteen meters closer to pop groups like Kraftwerk, KLF or the Sex Pistols than to our role models like Marcel Duchamp, Claes Oldenburg or Jacques Tati. Nowadays, instead of philosophising about art and art mechanisms, we'd rather sit together and smoke a pipe on it. Gymnastics interest us more. We do acrobatic splits between art, graphic design and advertising. Still, we don't know for certain what Büro Destruct is; people on the outside probably have a much more realistic idea of what we are. One thing is for sure. Büro Destruct is an eerie feeling.

During our training to become graphic designers back in the days, we had to work without computers and software. It was the old school technique of Chinese ink, the brush, the ruler and the ruling pen, which made designing fonts a real pain. It was only with the introduction of the computer that we found joy in creating fonts. Being able to type your own fonts on a keyboard and use them without restriction is a great motivation factor. This has nothing (or maybe only a little) to do with being lazy. In our opinion, it is a misconception that machines restrict one's freedom to create. We believe that working with machines is liberating. Not only because you're faster that way, but also because working with computers – as opposed to pen and paper – makes it easier to break the rules of design. Working beyond the rules only makes the rules more visible.

As Jean-Luc Godard sees himself as an organiser of image and sound, we see ourselves as organisers of image and letter. For us, painting and drawing is a form of search – the search that is probably pre-conditional to all forms of creative work. It is this search that leads us from one stroke or shape to the next stroke, the next shape. One thing leads to the other. It is a wonderful way of being close to oneself and people you like. This is the kind of «Holy Moment» we're looking for. One should always keep one's eyes on the nearest thing and not look too far ahead. As the learning process of a child takes a lot of patience, painting and drawing take a lot of patience too. Impatience is like poison for creativity.
One ought to take great pleasure in acting childish. Good painters that possess profound understanding of colour are childlike. They express what they feel. The beauty in this world is that it can be changed! To put it briefly: live. Arthur Rimbaud said, «No man has ever created anything.» The artist is unable to create. He can only re-arrange and re-organise things.
We ask for a lot of liberties. The liberty to act like jesters. A sort of freedom that has more to do with an insatiable quest for knowledge than with elitist bigotry. Even though the child Büro Destruct meanwhile wears a beard and may be a little older, it still wants to explore, learn and play. Playing has always stood right at the top of the list of priorities at Büro Destruct. Therefore we would not hesitate to put our names to the Pet Shop Boys statement «careerists are uncool.» In the end, our work is about individuality for the good of a collective identity. No carte blanche but a carte orange!

Especially in connection with our work, we feel deeply related to the people of the forests and the fairies of the meadows. From far away one can see the lights and hear the sounds. They're like a drum roll in a two quarter beat or possibly a little more. Like a whole lot more. Like fire in red, green and blue. And a little white. And a little black. A whole lot of the black and only very little of the white. Like a two quarter beat drum roll.

We are a whole bunch. A bunch of small people. People with short arms and short legs and big hearts. Somewhere right inside us. We are the people you don't see or don't usually see. We are the people that pull the cover over your head when you go to sleep and we are the people that stand by your side if the walls fall in on you. People that are really always there for you. Very close to you and at the same time far from you. We are your dreams. Dreams like a Technicolor movie or dreams in black and white. A whole lot of the black and only very little of the white. And from far away one can

ganze Menge mehr. Wie ein Feuer in rot, grün und blau. Und ein bisschen weiss. Und ein bisschen schwarz. So ganz viel von dem bisschen Schwarz und nur ganz wenig von dem Weiss. Wie ein Trommelwirbel im Zweivierteltakt.

Wir waren eine ganze Menge. Eine Menge kleiner Leute. Leute mit kurzen Armen und kurzen Beinen und grossen Herzen; irgendwo mittendrin in uns. Wir sind die Leute, die du nicht siehst oder die du nicht zu sehen pflegst. Wir sind diese Leute, die dir die Decke über den Kopf ziehen, wenn du einschläfst und wir sind diese Leute, die bei dir sind, wenn dir die Decke auf den Kopf fällt. Leute, die eigentlich immer für dich da sind. Ganz nah neben dir und gleichzeitig ganz weit weg von dir. Wir sind deine Träume. Träume wie ein Farbfilm in Technicolor oder Träume in Schwarz-Weiss. So ganz viel von dem Schwarz und nur ganz wenig von dem Weiss. Und von ganz weit weg kommen die Lichter und die Geräusche. Wie ein Trommelwirbel im Zweivierteltakt. Wir stehen ganz nah am Feuer.

Und wenn du uns heute fragst, wer wir sind, dann werden wir dir antworten. Wenn du uns heute fragst, wer wir sind, dann werden wir dir antworten:
«Wir sind die Leute, die du nicht siehst. Die Leute aus dem Wald. Die Leute mit den kurzen Armen und den kurzen Beinen. Die Leute, die dich in der Nacht besuchen, dir die Decke über den Kopf ziehen, die dir die Luft zum atmen nehmen. Wir sind die Leute, die dich auf weite Reisen schicken.»
Wenn du uns heute fragst, wer wir sind, dann werden wir dir antworten:
«Wir sind die Leute, die eigentlich immer für dich da sind.»

Und wenn wir auf den Boden gucken: Wenn wir auf den Boden gucken, dann sehen wir da die Blätter liegen, dann sehen wir da die Käfer kriechen, dann sehen wir da die Schnecken lieben. Ganz unten. Unter uns.
Kleines Blatt, du machst uns völlig platt. Süsses kleines Blatt, wenn wir dich sehen, dann lächelt unser Herz nur für dich. Deine Haut ist so zart. Kleiner Käfer, bleib wie du bist, du bist so schön und du kleine Schnecke bleib da. Bleib da und geh nicht weg!

Und wenn wir zu den Bäumen gucken: Wenn wir zu den Bäumen gucken, dann sehen wir Bäume wie aus einer anderen Welt. Bewachsen mit unförmigem Moos, übersäht von winzigen Hautblumen und musikalischen Figuren. Tief verankert mit einem komplizierten Wurzelwerk. Trotzdem scheint sich alles von den Bäumen zu lösen. Auch die Dinge die unbedingt festgehalten werden müssen. Die Dinge die uns wichtig erscheinen.

Und wenn wir zu den Räumen zwischen den Bäumen gucken: Wenn wir zu den Räumen zwischen den Bäumen gucken, dann sehen wir da die jungen Götter schweben. Diese jungen Götter sind praktisch, man kann alles Mögliche mit ihnen bewerkstelligen. Obstbäume pflanzen, Wasser kochen, Zigaretten anzünden. Diese jungen Götter duften auch fein. Nach Erde, nach Wasser und nach Tabak.

Und wenn wir ins helle Feuer gucken: Wenn wir ins helle Feuer gucken, dann sind da Bruchstücke von buntem Glas, leuchtende Muster, zahllose Zickzack-Linien und Statuen aus Zinn. Dann ist da roter Rauch, grüner Rauch und blauer Rauch. Mittendrin im Feuer. In der tintigen Nacht.

Das Telefon klingelt. Kurze Arme und kurze Beine haben wir. Im Gesicht ein weisser Bart, wuchernde Haare und ganz vorne dran bunte Blüten in 3D. Blüten in jeder Farbe. Nach den Blüten sind da kleine Räume. Kleine Räume auf der Schwelle zum Surrealismus. Räume in verschiedenen Formen. Rund, eckig, buchstabenförmig und so weiter, und so fort. Das Telefon klingelt. Und von ganz weit weg kommen die Lichter und die Geräusche. Wie ein Trommelwirbel im Zweivierteltakt. Wir stehen ganz nah am Feuer und es leuchtet hell. Rauchzeichen sieht man von weitem. In rot, in grün und in blau.

see the lights and hear the sounds. Like a two quarter beat drum roll. We stand close to the fire.

And should you ask us today who we are, we shall answer your question. Should you ask us today who we are, we shall say:
«We are the people you don't see. The people from the woods. The people with the short arms and the short legs. The people that visit you at night, that pull the cover over your head, to stop you from breathing. We are the people that send you on a long journey.»
Should you ask us today who we are, we shall reply:
«We are the people that are really always there for you.»

And if we look to the ground: If we look to the ground, we see the leaves lying there, we see the beetles crawl, we see the snails making love. Deep down. Below us.
Little leaf, you render us void. Sweet little leaf, if we look at you, our heart smiles just for you. Your skin is so delicate. Little beetle, stay as you are, you are full of beauty. And you, little snail, stay here. Be still and do not part!

And if we look up to the trees: If we look up to the trees, we see trees like from another world. Coated in moss, covered with tiny skin flowers and musical shapes. Rooted deep down with a complex root work. Even so, everything appears to part from the trees. Even the things that need holding on to. The things that seem important to us.

And if we look at the space between the trees: If we look at the space between the trees, we see young gods levitating. Those young gods are convenient; you can accomplish all sorts of things with them: plant fruit trees, boil water, light cigarettes. These young gods also have a lovely scent. The scent of earth, water and tobacco.

And if we look into the bright fire: If we look into the bright fire, we see fragments of colourful glass, lucid patterns, countless zigzag lines and statues of tin. There is red smoke, green smoke and blue smoke. Right inside the fire. In the pitch-black night.

The phone rings. Short arms and short legs we have. A white bearded face, rampant hair and at the very front there's blossoms in 3D. Blossoms in every colour. After each blossom there's small spaces. Small spaces at the verge of surrealism. Spaces in different shapes. Round, square, letter-shaped and so on and so forth. The phone rings. And from far away one can see the lights and hear the sounds. Like a drum roll – two quarter beat. We stand close to the fire – it shines so bright. One can see smoke signals from far away. In red, green and blue.

von/by HGB Fideljus   Translation by Kevin Mueller

«Breakin' Dwarf»
Character design

2003

Unpublished

BD:9

Small City
Clean Water

Small City
Less Stress

Small City
Cute People

Small City
Big Beats

Small City
Nice Cheese

**Small City
Less Pollution**

«Ten reasons
to work in a small
city like Berne»

2003

Unpublished

Small City
No Rush-Hour

**Small City
Better Friends**

**Small City
Huge Clients**

**Small City
Big Design**

«BD intim»
Digicam pictures
300x225pixel

1999-2003

www.burodestruct.net/
bd/room/intim.html

EVEREST

BD. ST. MORITZ
ABCDEFGHIJKLMN
OPQRSTUVWXYZ
1234567890

Left:
«BD St. Moritz»
Typedifferent Font

2003

www.typedifferent.com

BD:14

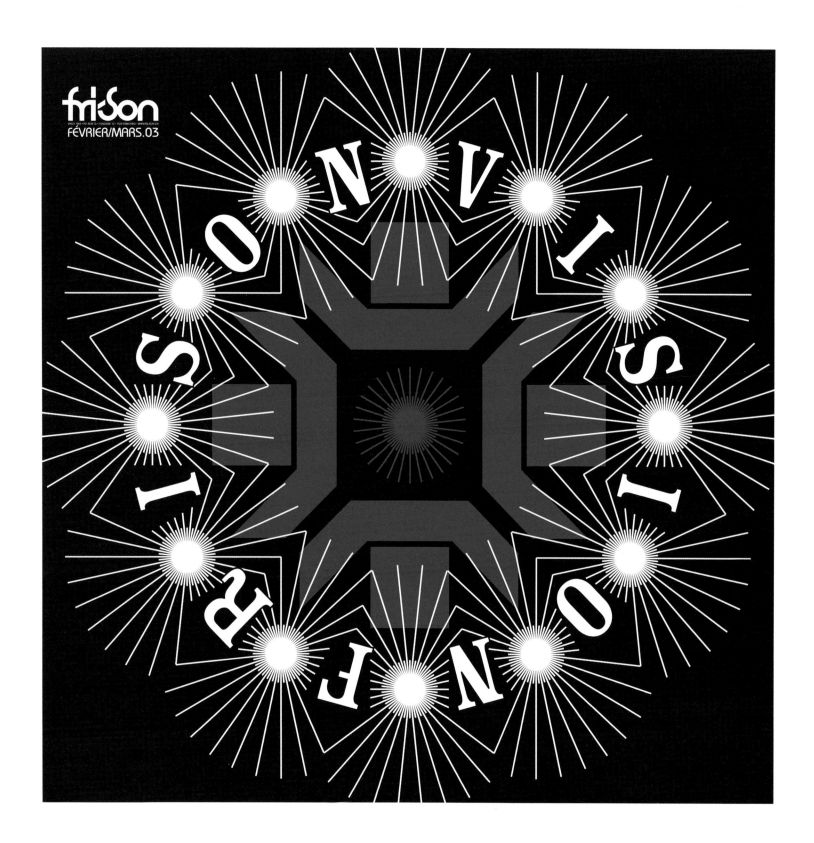

Left page top:
«Everest: Heimlich Maneuver»
LP- and CD-sleeve
313x313mm
120x120mm

Illustration of the Matterhorn,
Switzerland's most famous
mountain.

Client:
Everest

2002

Top:
«Fri-Son Eurovision»
Monthly programme poster
420x420mm

Client:
Fri-Son, Fribourg

2003

«Holy Moments»
Ingredients and results from
a cheese-fondue evening.

Right page:
«Fondue-Explosion»
Monthly programme poster
1280x980mm

Client:
Kulturhallen Dampfzentrale,
Bern

2003

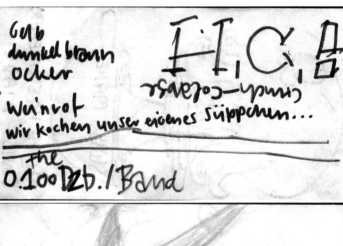

BD:17

«Swiss Expo Panorama»
Bricollage, Flash-animations

Swiss panoramas made with
snippets from traditional
swiss posters.

Client:
Expo02/Artix Club,
Biel/Bienne

2002

www.burodestruct.net/bd/
discotec/expomovies.html

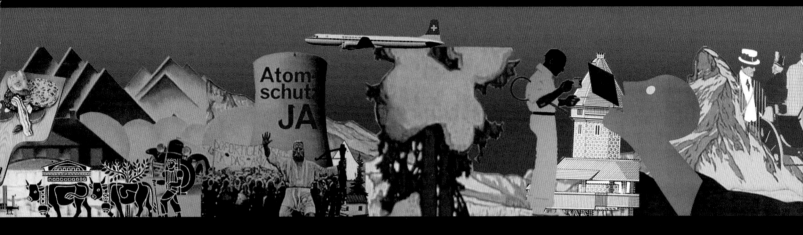

«büro destruct»
Crew portrait photo

Magazine Cover
Design Plex
Minna No Digital Design
Magazine
1/January No.57, 2002

Photo:
Regula Roost, Bern
Hair & Makeup:
Anja Wiegmann, Bern

Client:
Design Plex Magazine,
Japan

2001

Right page:
«Swiss Graphic Design»
Book cover & poster
240x300mm
840x1190mm

Client:
Die Gestalten Verlag,
Berlin

2000

BD:20

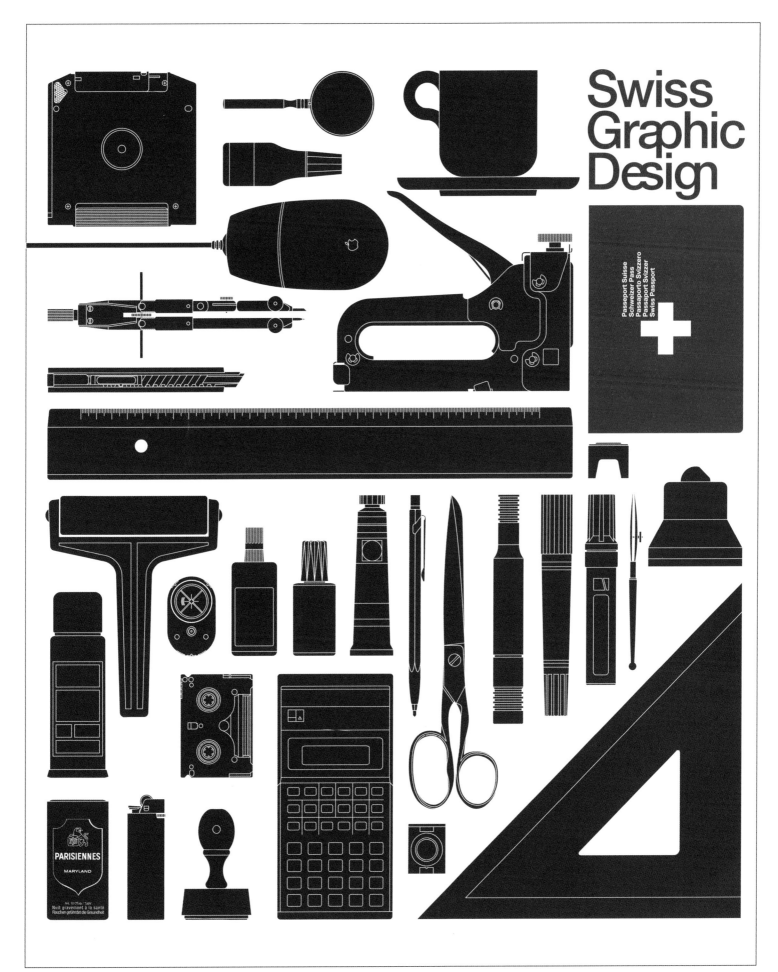

Swiss Graphic Design

«Swiss Graphic Design
Desaster»

2002

Unpublished

Left page:
«Bike Attack»
Illustration

Flyer and poster
for Bike event
210x297mm
500x700mm

Client:
Red Bull

2002

«Trailfox»
Illustration

Flyer and poster
for Bike event
210x297mm
500x700mm

Client:
Red Bull

2003

Bottom:
«Fuck you, Kawasaki is back!»
Advertisements for
Motorbikes

Client:
Aha Puttner Bates, Wien
Creative Director: Alexandra
Flotzinger-Ehrlich

2002

Top:
«Olmo Fashion»
Postcard for fashion party
148x105mm

Client:
Olmo, Bern

1999

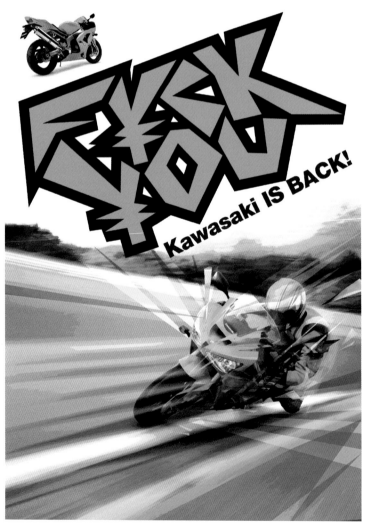

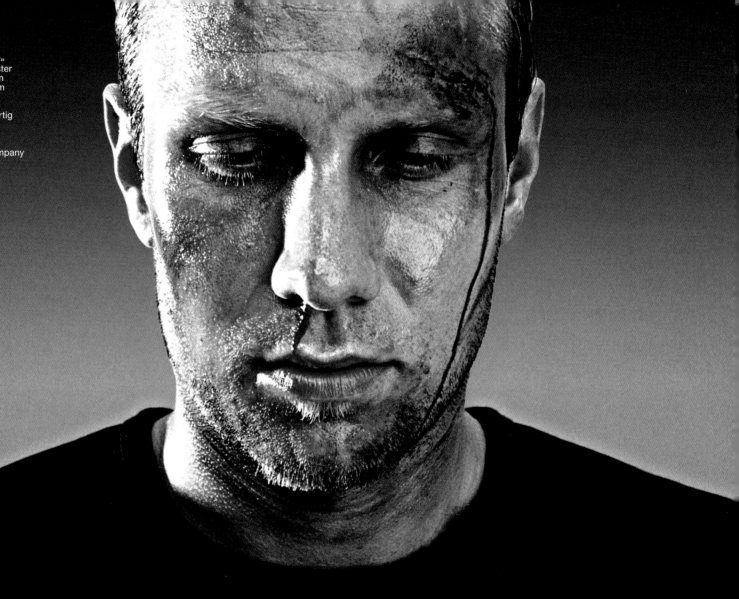

«Stuntwear»
Ad and poster
210x297mm
500x700mm

Photo:
Caspar Martig

Client:
Stuntwear
clothes company

2002

«Devilman The Revenge II»
Collage with video stills

Right:
«Stuntwear & Evilproduction»
Logotypes

Client:
Evilproduction
& Stuntwear
clothes company

1999-2003

Unpublished

«Devilman The Revenge II»
Collage with video stills

«Fritz Fertig»
Character illustration
for a magazine

Client:
UV UltraViolet
Magazine, Geneva

2003

BD:30

«Polar days»
Character design

2002

Unpublished

www.burodestruct.net/bd/
characters/

Top:
«Seven24»
Composings for ads
210x297

Client:
Swisscom Systems,
Contexta

2001

Bottom:
«Seven24 Runner Family»
3D character design

Client:
Swisscom Systems,
Contexta

2001

«Seven24, Servicerunner
and Robotrunner»
3D character design

Client:
Swisscom Systems,
Contexta

2001

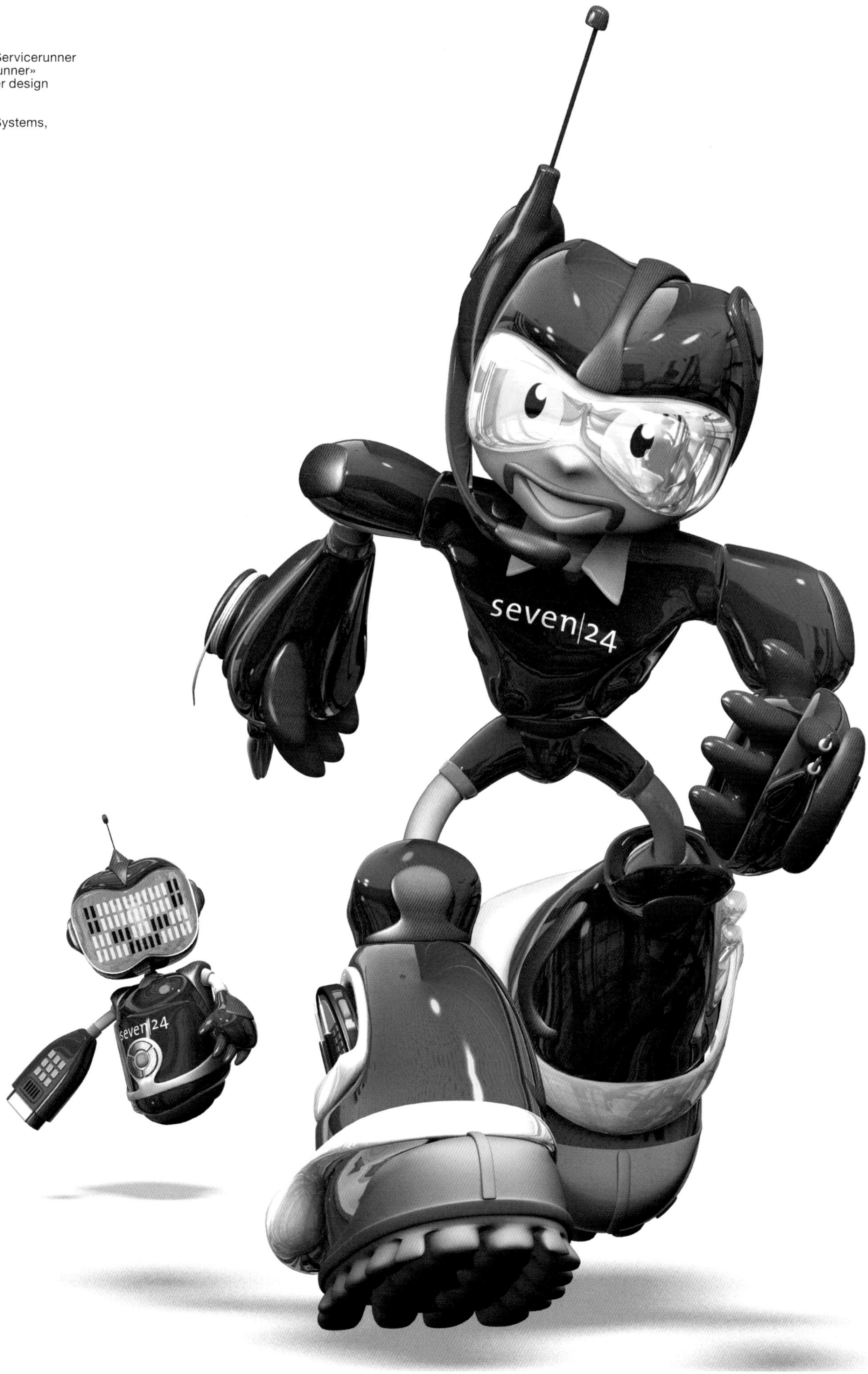

seven|24

seven|24

Top, left to right:
«Phant, Owsky, Rabbic,
Kangoo, Äisbär»
Character designs

2000-2003

www.burodestruct.net/bd/
characters/

«Owsky Invasion»
Character Design

2002

www.burodestruct.net/
bd/characters/mole.html

«Different cultures»
Illustration

2001
Unpublished

BD:35

Bottom:
«Eric Mingus»
Concert poster and flyer
420x420mm
120x120mm

Client:
Reitschule,
Bern

2000

Right:
Template from a website
for the Eric Mingus
illustration

Left:
«Tom Clark: King Tide»
LP- and CD-sleeve
313x313mm
121x121mm

Client:
Morris/Audio

2002

Bottom:
«Tom Clark»
Illustration
for LP- and CD-sleeve

Client:
Morris/Audio

2002

Unpublished

«Büne Huber:
Honigmelonemond»
CD-folder
384x115mm

Client:
BMG Ariola
(Schweiz) AG

2000

«Creatio Helvetica Chut!
Lärm, Bruit, Noise, Ruido»
Poster and magazine spread
2180x1500mm
480x330mm

Client:
Edition CH

2000

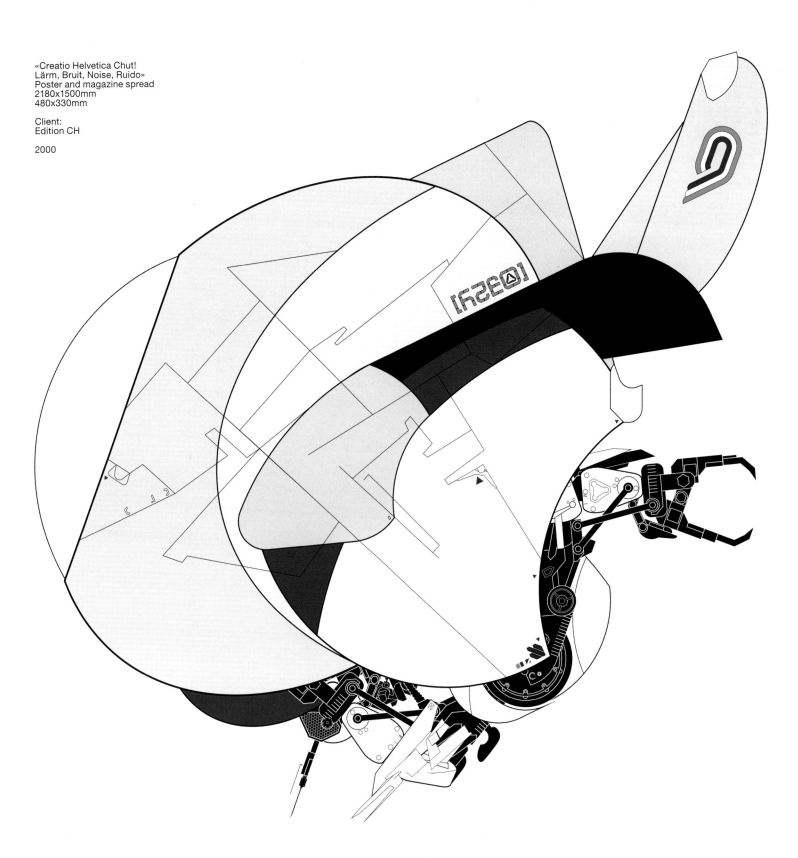

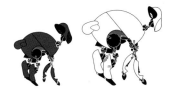

«Vision»
Outdoor rave
Flyer, poster, CD-sleeve
240x360mm
121x121mm

Client:
Dekadance,
Leila Benaissa

2002

«Rainbow»
Monthly programme
poster
700x1000mm

Client:
Kulturhallen
Dampfzentrale,
Bern

2000

Cyan   Magenta **Schwarz**

«Nevada»
Monthly programme
poster
700x1000mm

Client:
Kulturhallen
Dampfzentrale,
Bern

2000

«Burningman»
Photo-collage

2003

Unpublished

BD:44

BD:45

Bottom:
«Pürzliboum»
Stills from Rainbow movie

2001

RAINBOW
FOLLOW US

Rainbow

rainbow

Rainbow

Follow US

Rainbow

Rainbow

Left and right:
«Rainbow»
Sketches and final logotype

«BD Rainbow»
Typedifferent font

2000

www.typedifferent.com

Rainbow™
ABCDEFGHIJKLMNOPQRSTUVWXYZ
abcdefghijklmnopqrstuvwxyz
0123456789
(\)_!&'0ß,-./:;«»?@ÄäÖöÜü«»-Seøj

«All around and nowhere»

2003

Unpublished

BD:49

«EchoClub»
Poster and flyer
660x405mm
132x80mm

Photo: Kevin Mueller

Client:
CUE - Institute of
Contemporary Urban
Encounters

2002

www.urbanfields.net

BD:50

SAT
13-APRIL-2002
LOUNGE 22:00 / DANCEFLOOR 24:00-03.30
DJS SMAT (ELECTRO_SHOX) & KEV THE HEAD (MOUTHWATERING, CUE CENTRAL EUROPE)
METROPOLITAN ENVIRONMENT PROJECTED BY CUE

ECHO CLUB

KULTURHALLEN DAMPFZENTRALE BERN - CH

ECHO CLUB

ECHO CLUB LIVE

SAT
06-APRIL-2002
23:00
BENJAMIN WILD (FORCETRACKS/DIAL/KOMPAKT/FESTPLATTEN DE)
DJ DUSTBOWL (100 MOUTHWATERING MENUS INC. CH)

KULTURHALLEN DAMPFZENTRALE BERN - CH

ECHO CLUB LIVE

70

ECHO CLUB

SAT-12.02.2000 DJ SWO
SAT-11.03.2000 DJ SELECTAH J.
SAT-15.04.2000 DJ BOB@FETT

09:00-12:00PM LOUNGEBAR «BEYOND THE LOCAL EYE»
               PROJECTIONS BY CUE
00:00-03:30AM ELECTRONIC DANCEFLOOR (DJ'S SEE ABOVE)

KULTURHALLEN DAMPFZENTRALE BERN

«EchoClub»
Posters and flyers
660x405mm
132x80mm

Photo: Kevin Mueller

Client:
CUE - Institute of
Contemporary Urban
Encounters

2002/2000

www.urbanfields.net

«EchoClub»
Poster and flyer
660x405mm
132x80mm

Photo: Kevin Mueller

Client:
CUE - Institute of
Contemporary Urban
Encounters

2001

www.urbanfields.net

ECHO CLUB

KULTURHALLEN DAMPFZENTRALE BERN · CH

24-MAY-01   JAN JELINEK (SCAPE)
SUPPORTED BY DJ KEV THE HEAD
METROPOLITAN ENVIRONMENT PROJECTED BY CUE

ARE DEE (CHRONOX)
SUPPORTED BY DJ SWO
09-JUNE-01   METROPOLITAN ENVIRONMENT PROJECTED BY CUE

BD:53

frison

SINCE 1983 • PO BOX 15 • FONDERIE 13 • 1705 FRIBOURG • WWW.FRI-SON.CH

SEPTEMBER/OCTOBER

ma/di 24.09.2002 **READYMADE**

ve/fr 27.09.2002 FRI-SON DRUM'N'BASS AUTHORITIES PRESENT: **DJ BAILEY, VCA, DEEJAY MF, GEORGY GEE**

sa/sa 28.09.2002 **LE PEUPLE DE L'HERBE**

di/so 06.10.2002 **TOUCH LABEL NIGHT** FEATURING **FENNESZ, HAZARD, PHILIP JECK**

ve/fr 11.10.2002 **MAGMA**

sa/sa 12.10.2002 **SIGUR ROS WITH AMINA STRINGS**

ma/di 15.10.2002 **SCHNEIDER TM**

ve/fr 18.10.2002 **MARYGOLD, BLOTCH**

sa/sa 19.10.2002 **22-PISTEPIRKKO, BEAUTIFUL LEOPARD**

sa/sa 26.10.2002 **WATCHA, PLEYMO**

di/so 27.10.2002 **FREDERIC GALLIANO AND THE AFRICAN DIVAS**

«Aurelio»
and the Fontmonitor

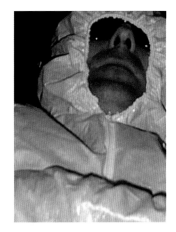

«Font ABC»
by Aurelio
made out of the BD
Beautiful Graphic Deliveries
sticker

1999

Unpublished

«Beautiful Graphic Deliveries»
Selfpromotion sticker
60mm

1999

Left page:
«Fri-Son»
Monthly programme
poster
420x420mm

Client:
Fri-Son,
Fribourg

2002

«Tatami-Garden»

Client:
Design Plex
Minna No Digital Design
Magazine, Japan
57/1 (last issue)

2002

3D Tatami

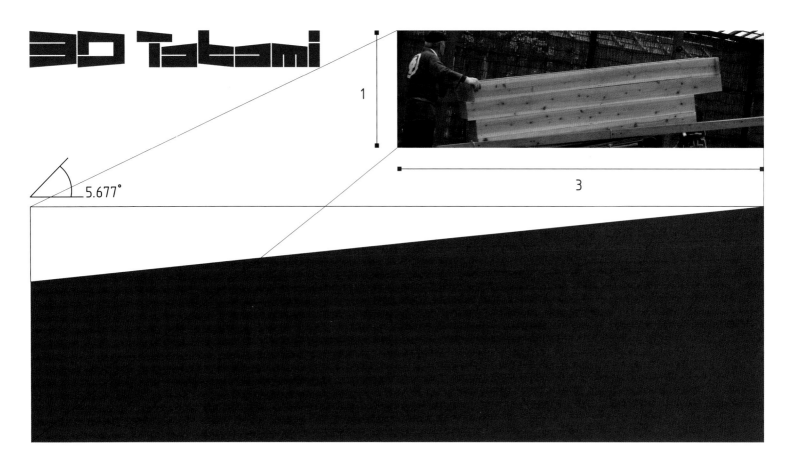

1

3

5.677°

Left page:
Tatami font inspiration

2003

Unpublished

«BD Tatami»
Typedifferent font

2001

www.typedifferent.com

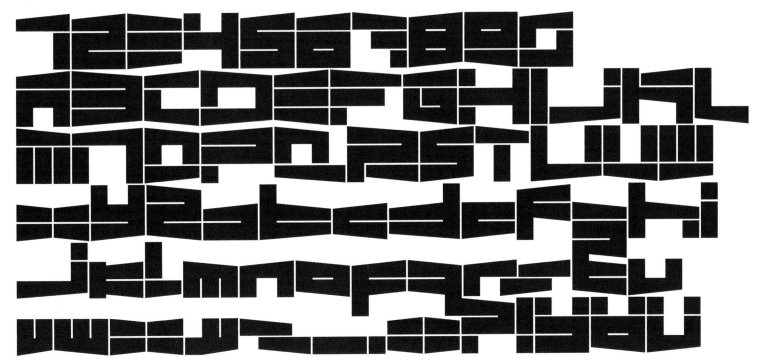

Right:
«Leftfield»
Concert poster and flyer
420x420mm
120x120mm

Client:
Mouthwatering Inc.

2001

Bottom:
Tatami font screensaver

www.typedifferent.com/
2001/goodies/tatami/
tatamisaver.html

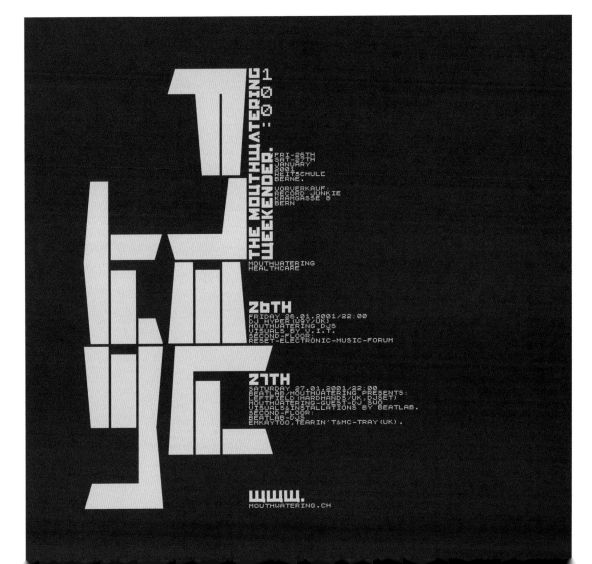

«Isolée»
Concert poster and flyer
420x420mm
120x120mm

Client:
Reitschule,
Bern

2001

Right page top:
«Koch»
Flyer for an art event
210x105mm

Client:
Olaf Holzapfel,
Dresden

2001

Right page bottom:
«Capital Bytes»
Clubnight flyer
148x105mm

Client:
International Students Club,
Bern

2000

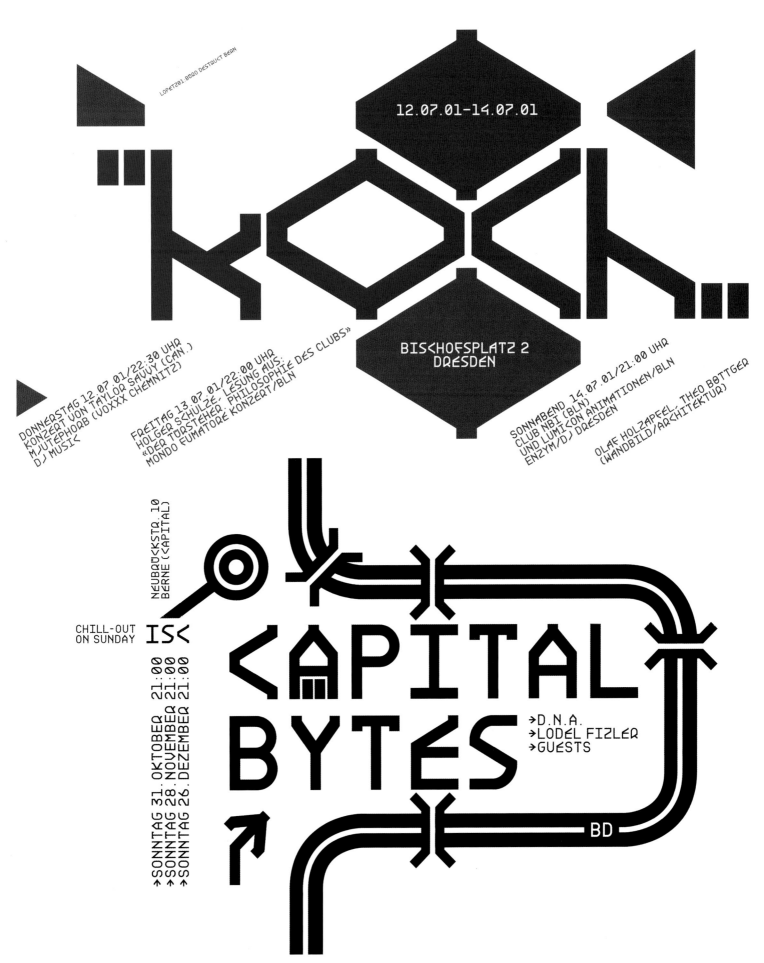

LOPET201 BODO DESTRUCT BEON

12.07.01–14.07.01

"kosk..."

BISCHOFSPLATZ 2
DRESDEN

DONNERSTAG 12.07.01/22:30 UHR
KONZERT VON TAYLOR SAVVY (CAN.)
MJUTEPHORB (VOXXX CHEMNITZ)
DJ MUSIC

FREITAG 13.07.01/22:00 UHR
HOLGER SCHULZE, LESUNG AUS:
«DER TÜRSTEHER. PHILOSOPHIE DES CLUBS»
MONDO FUMATORE KONZERT/BLN

SONNABEND 14.07.01/21:00 UHR
CLUB NBI (BLN)
UND LUMICON ANIMATIONEN/BLN
ENZYM/DJ DRESDEN

OLAF HOLZAPFEL, THEO BÖTTGER
(WANDBILD/ARCHITEKTUR)

NEUBRÜCKSTR. 10
BERNE (CAPITAL)

CHILL-OUT
ON SUNDAY   ISC

CAPITAL
BYTES

→D.N.A.
→LODEL FIZLER
→GUESTS

→SONNTAG 31.OKTOBER 21:00
→SONNTAG 28.NOVEMBER 21:00
→SONNTAG 26.DEZEMBER 21:00

BD

Top left:
«Modern Amusement»
Fashion event flyer
210x148mm

Client:
Kitchener,
Bern

2000

Middle left:
«Organic Grooves»
Concert flyer
148x105mm

Middle right:
«Domenico Ferrari»
Concert flyer
120x120mm

Client:
Kultrhallen
Dampfzentrale,
Bern

2001

Bottom left:
«Dj Vadim»
Concert flyer
159x60mm

Client:
Bogen 13,
Zürich

2001

«Drum'n'Brass»
Monthly programme
poster
1280x980mm

Client:
Kulturhallen
Dampfzentrale,
Bern

2002

KULTURHALLEN
DAMPFZENTRALE
WWW.DAMPFZENTRALE.CH

BD:63

«Grooverider»
Flyer and poster
for Drum'n'Bass clubnight
120x120mm
420x420mm

Client:
Reitschule, Bern

2001

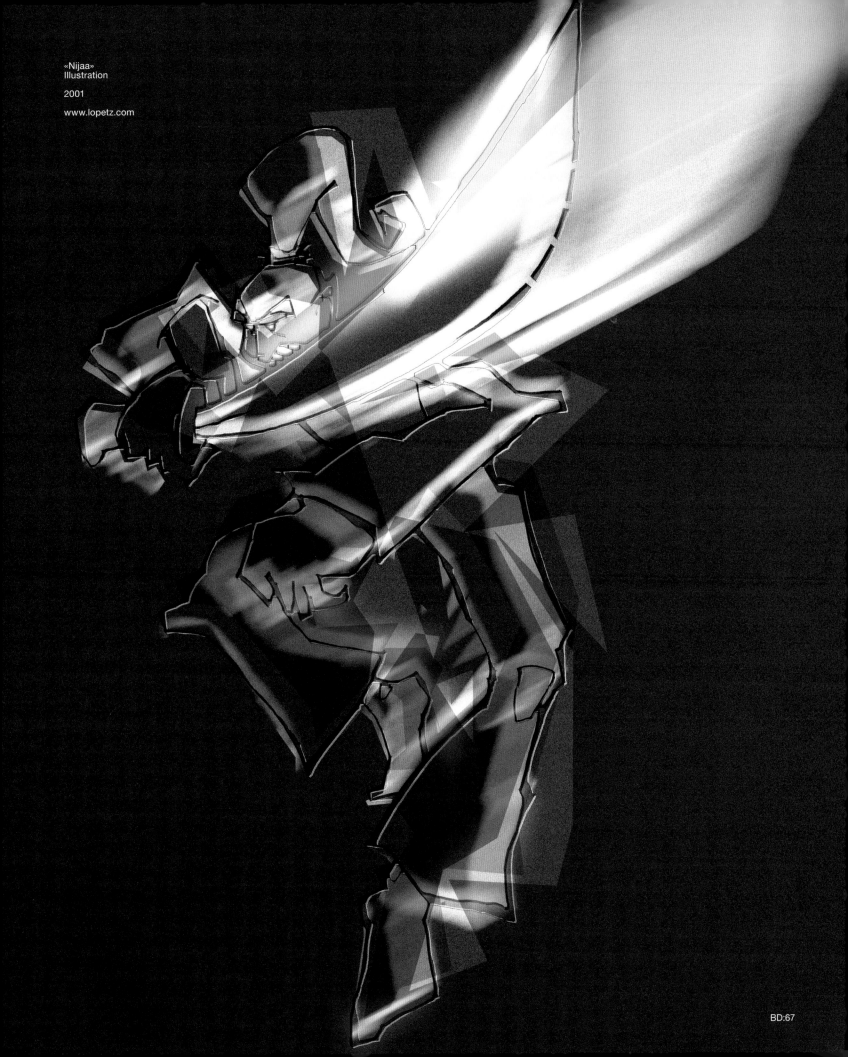

äbä	hiub
aberassle	housi
alütä	hüenerhutt
ankä	huerä
aschi	humpä
bärädräk	hüppere
bärätazä	hurti
bärn	iwärfä
bea	jäpsu
beiz	jöggu
böisi	läbäräplätzli
böögu	läckbobi
brättlä	lädelä
bräzäli	lamaschi
brönnär	lauerä
brüscht	liiribänz
büchsä	löru
büglä	loubä
bündig	lüüschä
bürzi	märku
chapä	mäuchä
charä	motzä
chäs	mudrig
chäschuächä	näggi
chätschä	nötli
chemifäger	obäusä
chemp	ömuscho
chessu	öpfumoscht
chischtä	pedä
chiubgigu	pennä
chiubi	peschä
chnubä	pfiffä
chnuschti	pflotsche
chodär	pfüderi
chöie	puderä
chotzä	pumpi
choubächlemär	pürzliboum
chrampfä	rippsär
chratzä	rithaue
chraue	röbu
chreisu	röschti
chrigä	rotzä
chue	roubrättlä
chümi	roukä
chüngu	runggle
chunschou	sackmässer
chuttä	sänf
chuttlä	sänkloch
däich	sapperlot
dänggälä	sargnagu
echli	schafsecku
egschtäsi	schiffä
fagantepack	schiffärä
fahnä	schigge
färlimore	schissä
finkä	schlärpälä
fleischmoudi	schleglä
fötälä	schlööflä
fotzuhung	schmiärlatz
fränä	schnäbichätschär
frässä	schnädderfräsig
freesä	schnägä
friisä	schnuddercheib
frittä	schnuderi
füdlä	schober
füdleblesch	schoggi
fummlä	schöppelimungi
furzä	schuttä
fuslä	secku
gaffe	seifächischtä
gafferahmdeckäli	snöber
gagu	souguet
gingä	souhung
ginggä	spüele
gitzi	stämpärätä
glungä	stemmbögelä
gmüätläch	stinkä
gnaggi	stutz
gnietig	süggu
goggi	suufä
golä	teigaffä
gömär	töggelä
gopf	totsch
gorpsä	tschinggä
gottlett	tschirggä
gramüsälä	tschirgge
granium	tutäublase
gschobe	vercheibät
gschweuti	vo bärn
gschwing	voglä
güetzi	voudurä
güggu	wäselig
gummiadlär	wäuebrättlä
gummiboum	widdlä
güppli	wixär
händi	wixbirä
härdöpfu	zahlegaa
häremechä	zigi
hegu	ziibä
henä	züpfä
henusode	züpfä

«Büro Discotec
Tokyo vs Bern»
Poster and flyer
420x420mm
120x120mm

2000

www.burodestruct.net/bd/
discotec.html

БЬЯО ビュロ ディスコテック
DISCOTEC

FREITAG 5.MAI 2000/22:30
FOYER INTERNATIONAL
KULTURHALLEN DAMPFZENTRALE BERN
D.N.A (ISC, BE) / LODEL FIZLER & HGB FIDELJUS (BD BE)
RAINBOW (BE) / LIA B & NAT (BE/GE)
VIDEOSBEAMS:BERNE CAPITAL CITY

WWW.BURODESTRUCT.NET/BD/DISCOTEC.HTML

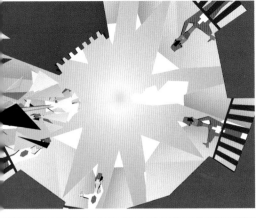
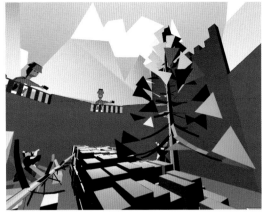
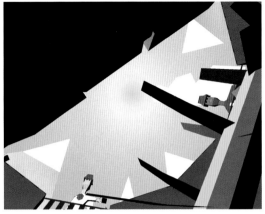

Top:
«Büro Discotec»
Vrml animations

Bottom:
«Future Sounds» and «Tanzart»
Vrml animations

1999-2001

www.ddd.ch

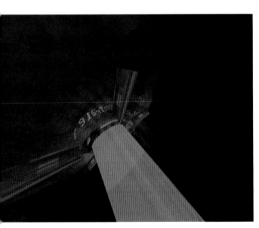

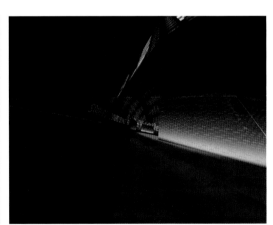

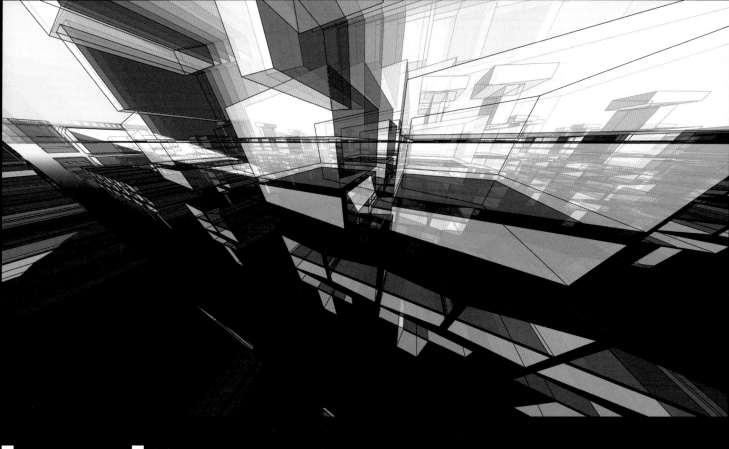

typotown

«TypoTown»
Shockwave application
and screensaver

2002
www.burodestruct.net/bd/
typotown/

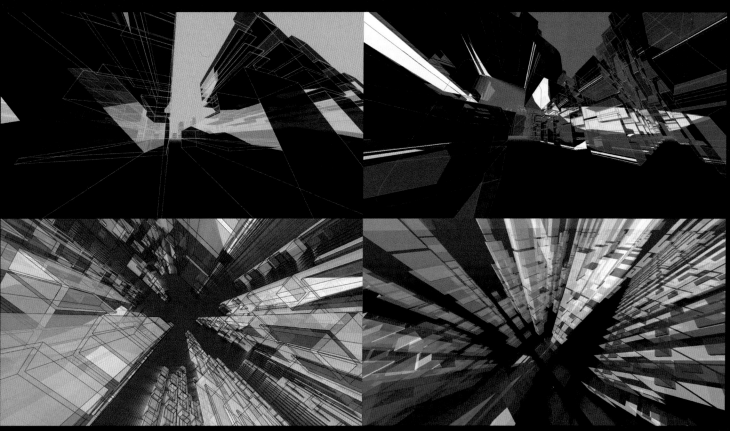

«Ereignisse»
Programme poster and flyer
for art-performance
featuring Roman Signer
700x1000mm
120x120mm

Client:
Kulturhallen Dampfzentrale,
Bern

2002

BD:73

BD:74

«Afronaut»
Illustration
for exhibition catalogue
Geld & Wert / Money & Value
280x240mm

Client:
Nüssli Special Events,
Expo.02

2002

Unpublished

**THURSDAY
13. APRIL 2000 21:00**

BroadCast UK

**REITSCHULE
DACHSTOCK BERN**

DJ KEV THE HEAD
VORVERKAUF: RECORD JUNKIE, KRAMGASSE 8, BERN

«Broadcast»
Concert poster and flyer
420x420mm
120x120mm

Client:
Reitschule, Bern

2000

«Humanoid Robot»
Sketches

Client:
Sony Robotics
Entertainment,
Japan

2001

Unpublished

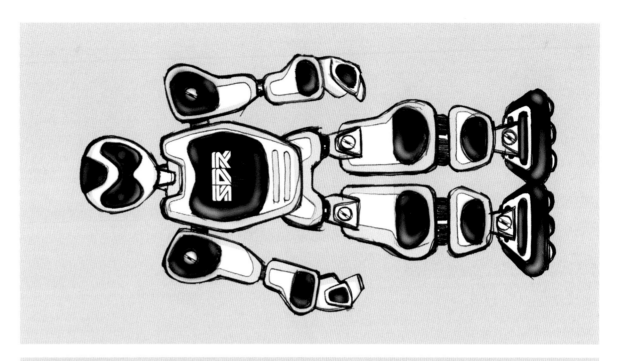

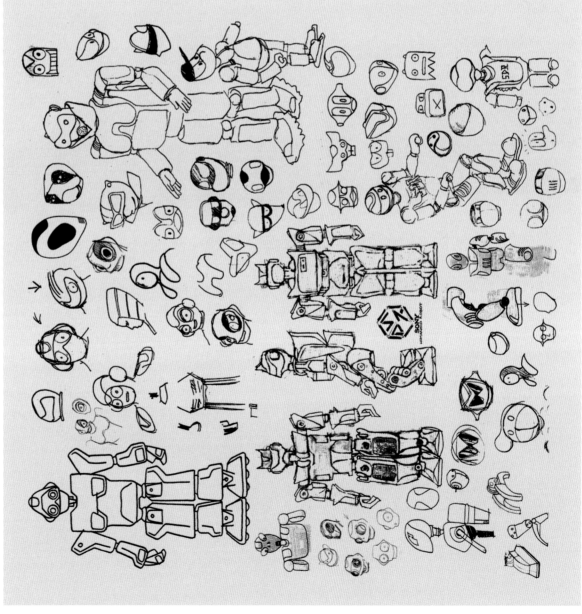

SONY
SDR
HUMANOID ROBOT

Top:
«SDR Humanoid Robot»
Logotype proposal

Bottom:
«Relaxed posing»
3D character design

Client:
Sony Robotics
Entertainment,
Japan

2001

Unpublished

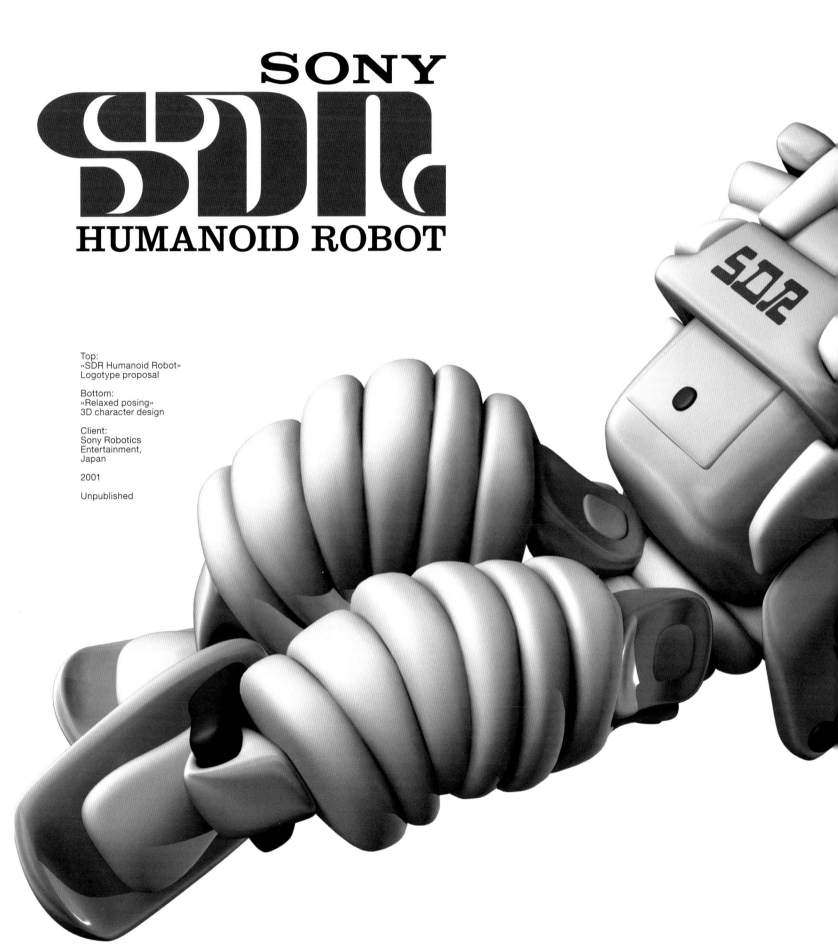

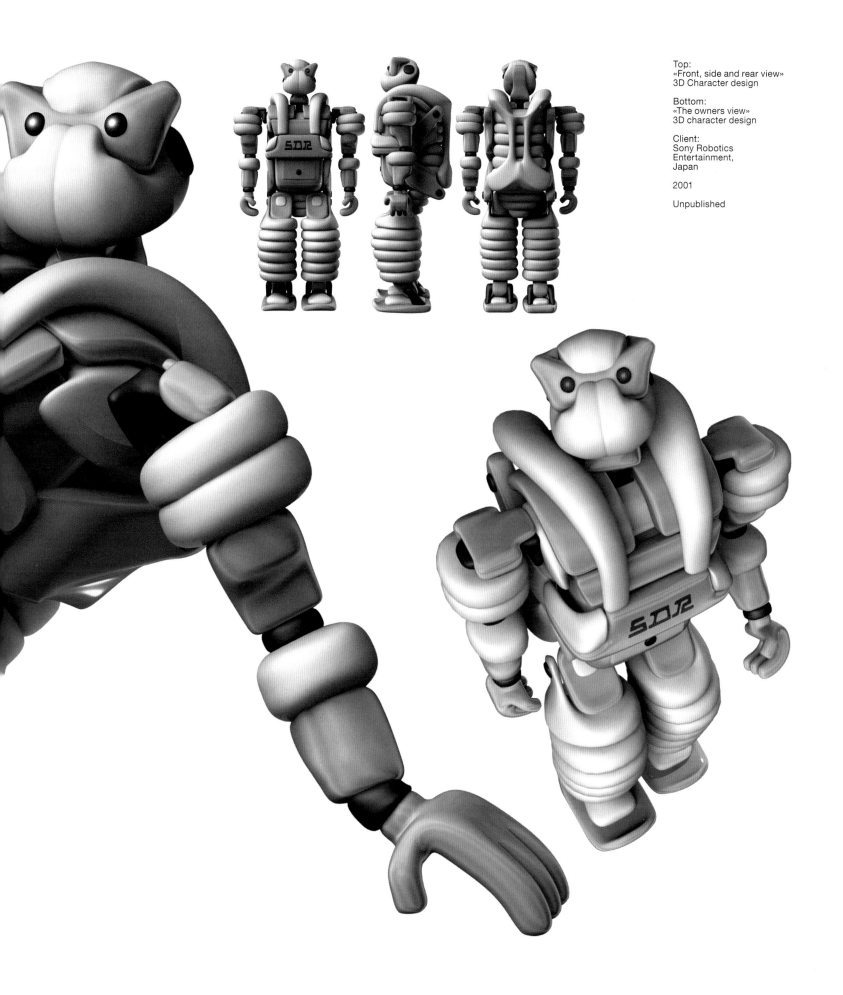

Top:
«Front, side and rear view»
3D Character design

Bottom:
«The owners view»
3D character design

Client:
Sony Robotics
Entertainment,
Japan

2001

Unpublished

«Ball Head»
Monthly programme
poster during the soccer
worldcup 2002
700X1000mm

Client:
Kulturhallen
Dampfzentrale,
Bern

2002

«Young Boys – Big Balls»
Fan-logotype
for Bern local soccer
club «Young Boys»

2002

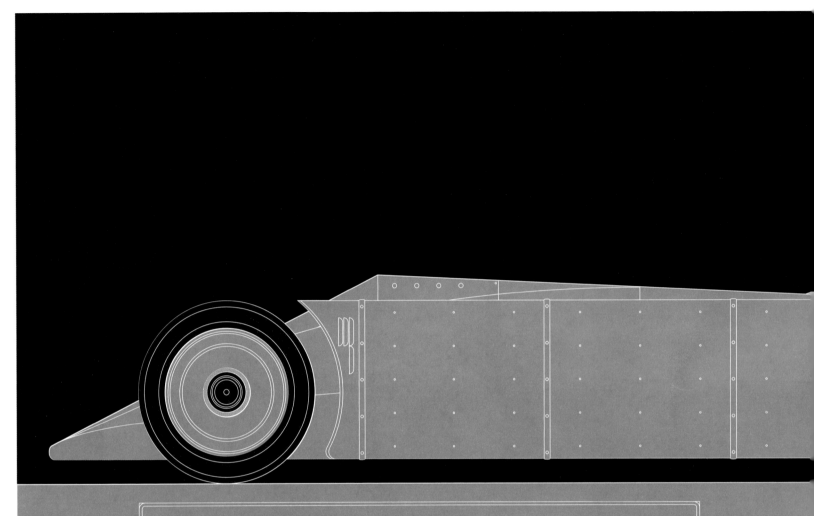

The Golden Arrow was designed by J.S. Irving and used a Napier Lion aero-engine of the Special 930bhp Schneider Trophy Type.
The twelve cylinders were in a W formation.
The car's low line design was achieved by the use of twin propeller shafts each side of the driver.

With the Golden Arrow, Sir Henry Segrave cracked the land speed record of 231.362mph (372.341kph) at Daytona Beach Florida on 11th March 1929. He died on the 13th of June 1930 when he was crack the water speed record (101.11mph) with his boat Miss England II on Lake Windermere in the UK.

Top:
«Golden Arrow»
Illustration for exhibition
catalogue
Geld & Wert/Money & Value
560x240mm

Client:
Nüssli Special Events,
Expo.02

2002

Unpublished

golden arrow

Sir Henry Segrave 1896-1930

bd colonius

abcdefghijklmnopqrstuvwxyz
abcdefghijklmnopqrstuvwxyz
0123456789(\)_?!"#/&'()*+,-.;:<=>^`
@·´¨äåöòüùøçœ¥¢ø//.,¿i«»–|ʊʁ©~
áâàãäéêèëíîìïñÑóôòõúûùæœßÆ

«BD Colonius»
Typedifferent Font

2002

www.typedifferent.com

«Balduin»
Illustration for LP- and
CD-sleeve

Client:
Crippled Dick Hot Wax,
Berlin

2002

www.bermuda.ch/balduin

Unpublished

«Instant Coffee»
Posters for Tekko exhibition,
Toronto
700x1000mm

2001

www.tekko.ca

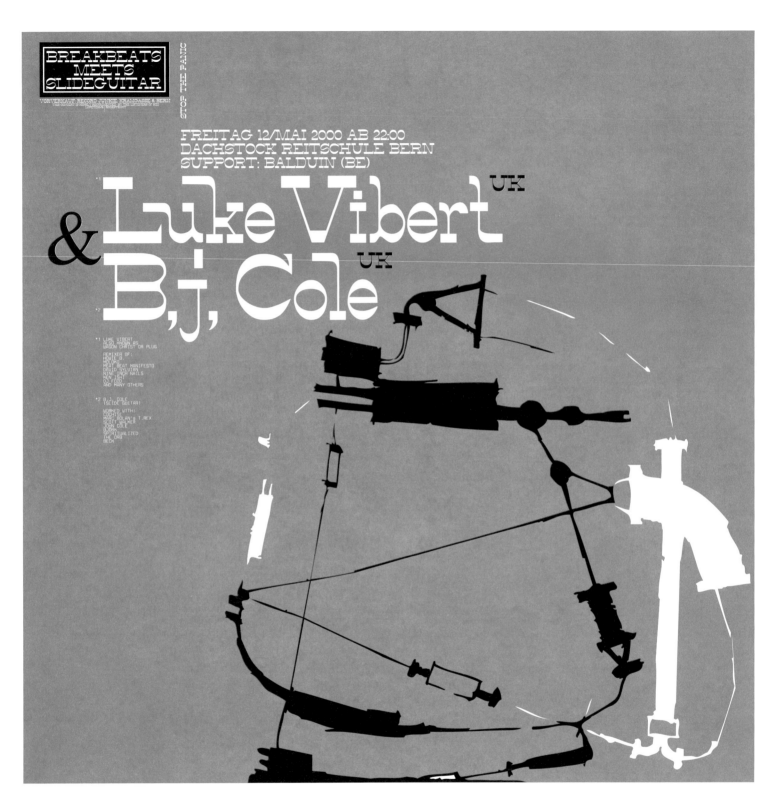

«Luke Viber & B.J. Cole»
Concert poster and flyer
420x420mm
120x120mm

Client:
Reitschule,
Bern

2001

«Büro Discotec Western»
Poster and flyer
420x420mm
120x120mm

Bottom left:
«Saloon Door Animation»
for Büro Discotec Western

2001

www.burodestruct.net/
bd/discotec.html

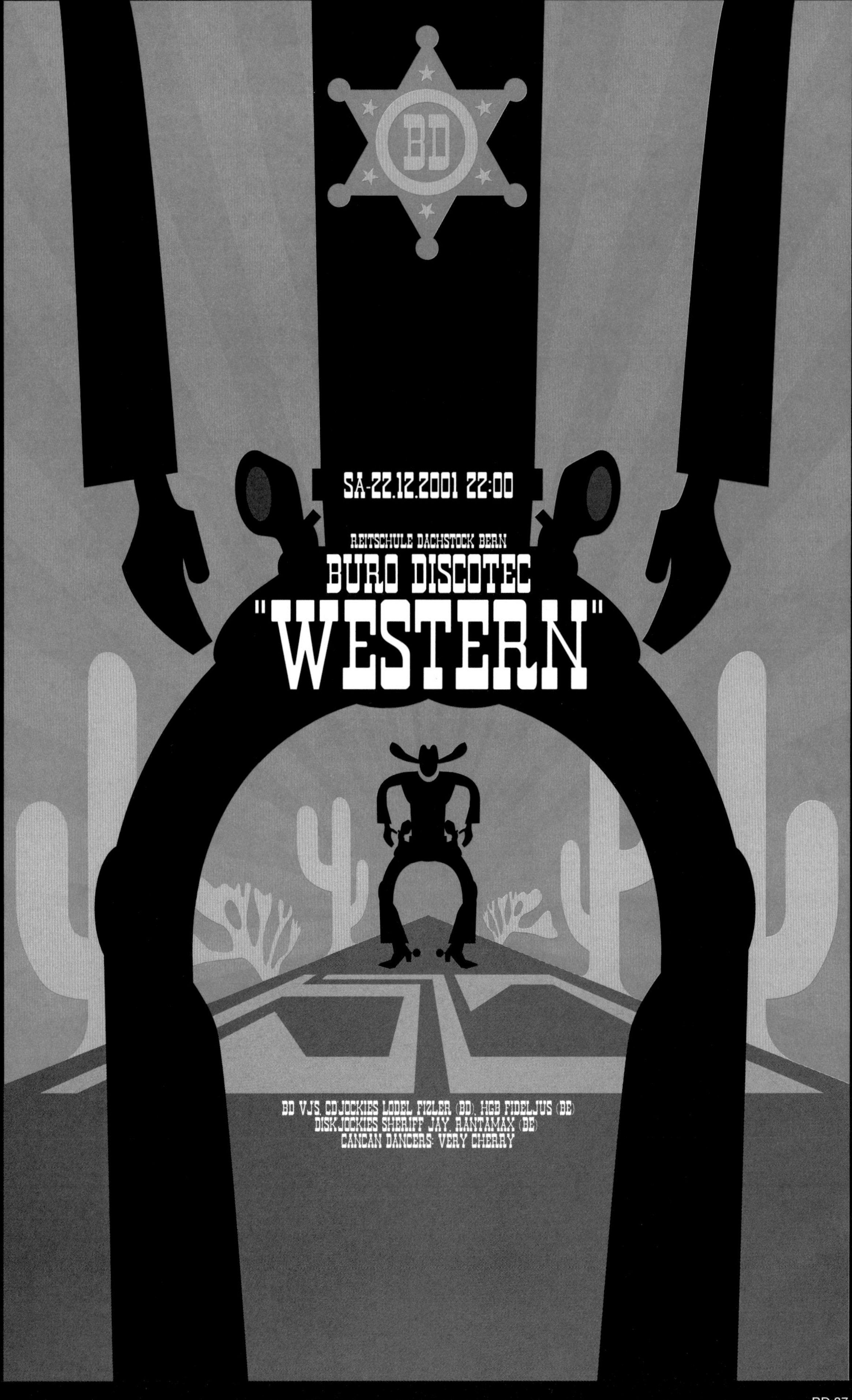

SA-22.12.2001 22:00

REITSCHULE DACHSTOCK BERN

BURO DISCOTEC

"WESTERN"

BD VJS CDJOCKIES LODEL FIZLER (BD), HGB FIDELJUS (BE)
DISKJOCKIES SHERIFF JAY, RANTAMAX (BE)
CANCAN DANCERS: VERY CHERRY

Highsoon |||||▌

«BD:Fossilworld»
Installation for the
Contemporary
Culture Convetion
exhibition
1000x1000mm

2002

Unpublished

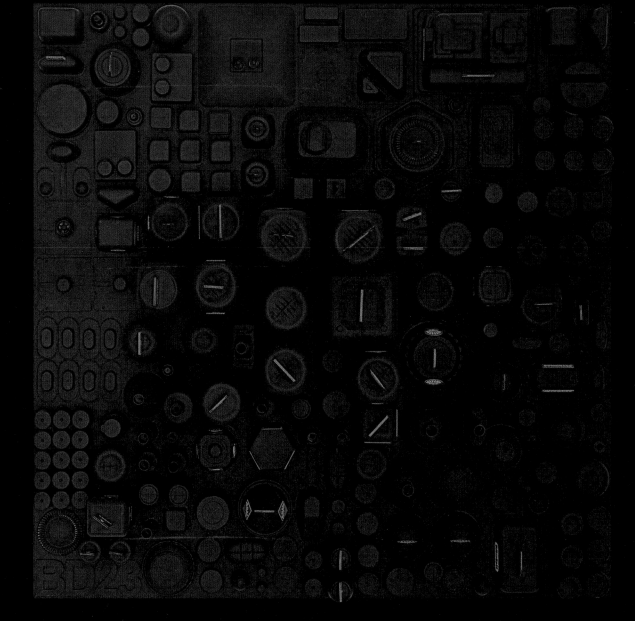

«Metropolitan Slave»
Illustration

2003

Unpublished

BD:91

«BD Hell»
Typedifferent font

2002

www.typedifferent.com

POEM

CBGBS

PUNK

TELEVISION

TOM VERLAINE

TIME

JOHN LYDON

ARTHUR RIMBAUD
1854-1891

RICHARD HELL

WILLIAM S BORROUGHS

THE VOIDOIS

CHARLES

PRETTY VACANT

BAUDELAIRE
1821-1867

BLANK GENERATION

HOT AND COLD   HEARTBREAKERS

PRETTY VACANT

SELF DESTRUCTION

PRETTY VACANT

JOHNNY THUNDER

MAL

SE

SID VICIOUS

BD HELL

ABCDEFGHIJKLMNOPQRSTUVWXYZ

ABCDEFGHIJKLMNOPQRSTUVWXYZ

RI

0123456789..:,;<=>?@«»/ÄÖÜ!#$%&[]*+-—=

YE£★°•ß®©™_''''1977

WATCH OUT PUNK IS COMING! PUNK PUNK PUNK PUNK SUPER PUNK Is not DEAD ROTTEN SID VICIOUS SEX PISTOLS SEX PISTOLS SEX PISTOLS SEX PISTOLS Pretty Vacant

ANARCHIE ASSHOLE fuck off CHAOS NO FUTURE No Future DESTROY The Damned NO BRAIN SUCKS

1977

77★

THERESA STERN

AREN

PISTOLS

ANDY WARHOL

RD HELL

RICHARD HELL

RAMONES

HELL

HELL

RICHARD HELL SUPERPUNK!

HELL HEEL

ARD HELL

HELL HELL

HELL HELL HELL

HELL

HELL

HELL

THERESA STERN

HELL

«DUBSelection #01»
CD-sleeve
120x120mm

2001

Unpublished

h1DUBSELECTION#01/2001

01:Azure Taint:Brainbow 8:02
02:Dr.Scissors:Luxor 6:04
03:Signal Theory:Egypt Dub 7:45
04:Futuristic Dub Foundation:Wakoom 6:42
05:Serious Smokers:Revolution in Ras 4:56
06:Benjamin Wild:Außenliegend24 6:15
07:Smith&Mighty:Move your Run 5:53
08:DubPlates from the Elephanthouse:Babylon Dub 3:55
09:Funkstar de Luxe feat Bob Marley:Sun is shining 6:08
10:Dillinger:Cocain In My Brain 6:15

DUB

← STEREO →

Brainblow™

1:UFO:Mothership 4:42
2:Neotropic:Aloo Gobi 5:45
3:ORB:Close Encounters 10:27
4:Finger:The Third Eye 5:52
5:Roots Manuva:Witness 4:12
6:Nightmares on Wax:Blou my Mind 3:22
7:Tweak:Playin Cool 5:49
8:Canto Azul:A Factor 6:16
9:Renegade Soundwave:Brixton 7:18
10:Freddy Fresh:Radio Budapest 5:18
11:Elec.Inpho:Lana De Rosa 5:51

← SPHEREO →

«Mothership Spaceselection»
CD-sleeve
120x120mm

2003

Unpublished

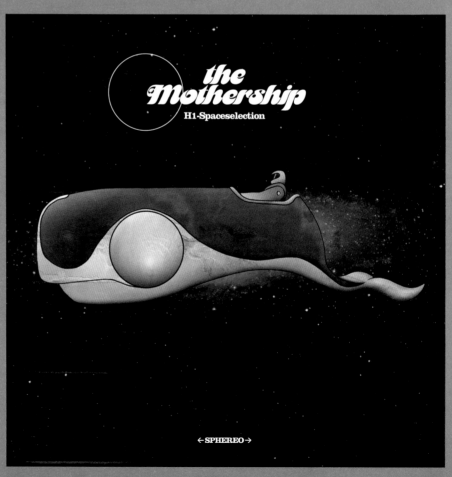

the Mothership
H1-Spaceselection

← SPHEREO →

«KD Kapitän»
Monthly programme
poster
905x1280mm

Client:
Kulturhallen
Dampfzentrale,
Bern

2003

«15 Jahre KD»
Monthly programme
poster
700x1000mm

Client:
Kulturhallen
Dampfzentrale,
Bern

2002

«Androidin»
Illustration
White tempera on
shampoo ad

1993

Unpublished

«Auawirleben.02»
Theater programme
and poster
210X592mm
700X1000mm

Client:
Berner Ensemble

2002

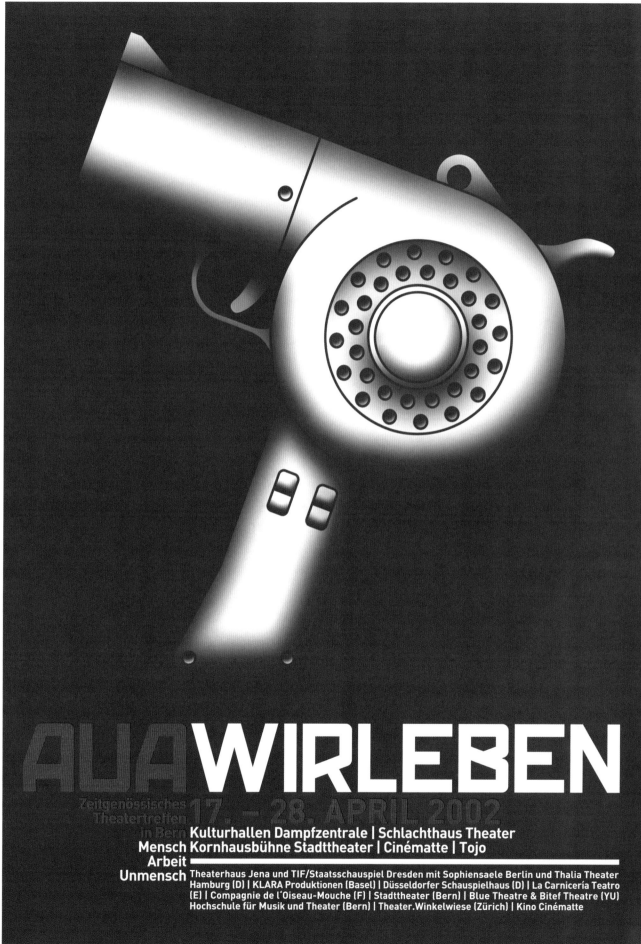

AUAWIRLEBEN

Zeitgenössisches
Theatertreffen 17. – 28. APRIL 2002
in Bern **Kulturhallen Dampfzentrale | Schlachthaus Theater**
Mensch **Kornhausbühne Stadttheater | Cinématte | Tojo**
Arbeit
Unmensch **Theaterhaus Jena und TIF/Staatsschauspiel Dresden mit Sophiensaele Berlin und Thalia Theater**
Hamburg (D) | KLARA Produktionen (Basel) | Düsseldorfer Schauspielhaus (D) | La Carnicería Teatro
(E) | Compagnie de l'Oiseau-Mouche (F) | Stadttheater (Bern) | Blue Theatre & Bitef Theatre (YU)
Hochschule für Musik und Theater (Bern) | Theater.Winkelwiese (Zürich) | Kino Cinématte

09.11.02
22:00 friSon

ANDREW WEATHERALL/UK
[TWO LONE SWORDSMEN/R.G.C./WARP]

RADIOACTIVE MAN/UK
AKA KEITH TENNISWOOD (LIVE)
[TWO LONE SWORDSMEN/R.G.C./WARP]

+FELDERMELDER (DEGADRON
+ELECTRIC SHEEP (DEGADRON
+VISUALS BY NEURONAUT

EINTRITT: 25.-

«Andrew Weatherall
& Radioactive Man»
Concert poster
420x420mm

Client:
Fri-Son, Fribourg

2002

BD:100

«GamePlex»
Logotag

Design Plex
Minna No Digital Design
Magazine
3/March No.47, 2001

Client:
Design Plex Magazine,
Japan

2001

Top left:
«Narita Inspected»
Book cover
240x280mm

Japan Graphic Design
Compiler by BD
ISBN# 3-931126-61-7

Published by
Die Gestalten Verlag, Berlin

2001

www.burodestruct.net/bd/
narita-uploaded/

Top right:
«Narita Inspected»
Logotype

Middle:
Original airport
X-ray images
of the bag with
the equipment
of a graphic designer.

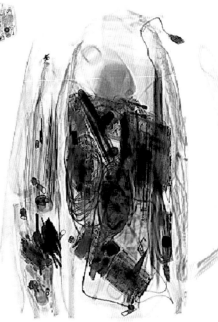

Photos from left to right: Heiwid, Yan, Ani (Nendo) and his wife Naho, Rockstar, Aya, Coffee House Fong, Komatsu, Hanzawa, Junko from Power Graphixx, Shin from 3kg, Mayumi (ex Shift), Lopetz, Sav-wo, Lopetz, Yan, Ryuko (ex DesignPlex), Kitai-san from Devilrobots.

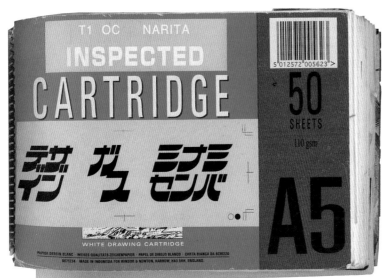

Left: The collection booklet with the «Kiribari Pages» including the original airport sticker «Narita Inspected»

FOREWORD FOR NARITA INSPECTED
THE JAPANESE LIVE IN THE FUTURE. COMPARED TO
EUROPE THEY ARE AHEAD BY SEVEN HOURS, TO AMERICA
THE DIFFERENCE CLOCKS IN AT AN IMPRESSIVE SIX-
TEEN HOURS. THE ADVANTAGE SEEMS SLIGHT BUT
REMAINS DECISIVE – THE MONIKER «LAND OF THE
RISING SUN» IS BY NO MEANS A COINCIDENCE. THIS
KIND OF REASONING IS A LITTLE SILLY, OF COURSE,
NOT TO BE DISMISSED. ON THE OTHER HAND, IS THE
FACT THAT A NEW STRAIN OF GRAPHIC DESIGNERS HAS
EMERGED FROM THIS CRADLE OF ELECTRONIC AND TECH-
NOLOGICAL PROGRESS, NURTURED DIRECTLY AT THE
SOURCE OF BRAND NEW ELECTRONIC ENTERTAINMENT
AND INFOTAINMENT. AND THIS IS VERY MUCH REFLEC-
TED BY THEIR WORK. IN A COUNTRY WHERE IT IS
COMMON TO SEE GROWN-UP ADULTS OBSESSING OVER
THEIR GAMEBOY ADVANCED DURING TRAIN JOURNEYS
OR CONSIDERING CHARACTERS WE WOULD HAVE
BANISHED TO THE NURSERY REALLY CUTE, VISUAL
LANGUAGE HAS ALWAYS HAD A LONG AND IMPORTANT
TRADITION.

BY USING THREE DIFFERENT «ALPHABETS», KANJI,
HIRAGANA AND KATAKANA AS WELL AS A JAPANISED
ENGLISH CALLED ROMAJI, THE JAPANESE ARE TRAINED
FROM BIRTH TO QUICKLY DISTINGUISH THE SUBTLE
VISUAL DIFFERENCES IN LETTERS THAT, TO US WEST-
ERNERS, SEEM INCREDIBLY COMPLEX AND UNFATHO-
MABLE. THEY HAVE BEEN BROUGHT UP WITH A SENSE
FOR DETAIL. AND THIS OBSESSION IS UBIQUITOUS
IN JAPANESE GRAPHIC DESIGN, SIMULTANEOUSLY
CLASHING WITH THE AESTHETIC TRANSLATION OF
ABSTRACTION AND REDUCTION. THIS IS A TRAIT NORM-
ALLY ASSOCIATED WITH SWISS GRAPHIC STYLES,
WHERE SIMILAR VIRTUES RULE: PATIENCE AND DILI-
GENCE IN SEARCH OF PERFECTION. FOR EXAMPLE,
THE JAPANESE CHERISH THEIR BUSINESS CARDS, TO
BE HANDED OVER POLITELY WITH BOTH HANDS –
FIGURATIVELY THIS IS HOW THEY SUBMITTED THEIR
GRAPHIC FILES FOR THIS BOOK.

WITH THIS BOOK I ATTEMPT TO CONVEY A POIGNANT
INSIGHT, NOT A COMPREHENSIVE OVERVIEW. IN TOKYO
ALONE THERE ARE AT LEAST THREE TIMES AS MANY
GRAPHIC DESIGNERS AS IN ALL OF SWITZERLAND.

BESIDES PRESENTING EXAMPLES FROM 33 DIFFERENT
STUDIOS MY MAIN CONCERN WAS TO PROVIDE A SNEAKY
GLIMPSE OF THE JAPANESE WORK ENVIRONMENT AND
VISUAL SURROUNDINGS.

DUE TO LACK OF SPACE AND EXORBITANT RENTS A LOT
OF YOUNG GRAPHIC DESIGNERS WORK FROM HOME, WITH
LAPTOP AND NET ACCESS WITHIN THEIR PRIVATE
COLLECTORS HEAVEN. A VISIT TO A JAPANESE STUDIO
WILL OFTEN TRIGGER A SPEEDY TIDYING SESSION BY
THE OWNERS. ON THIS OCCASION, I WOULD LIKE TO
EXTEND A VERY WARM THANK YOU TO ALL THE PARTI-
CIPANTS. THEY HAVE ALLOWED US AN EXCITING PEEK
AT JAPANESE LIFE AND GRAPHIC DESIGN.

↑ 5.5 PT

FR 01.10 - SO 31.10
KULTURHALLEN DAMPFZENTRALE

BDR MONO
ABCDEFGHIJKLMNOPQRSTUVWXYZ
ABCDEFGHIJKLMNOPQRSTUVWXYZ
0123456789
[\]^_`!"#%&´()*+,-./:;<=>
?@äÄÅØØÜÜØ¢£¥€$↙←↓→↑
%¿¡«»–"2331˜°□®©™

THE QUICK BROWN FOX JUMPS OVER A LAZY DOG.
THE QUICK BROWN FOX JUMPS OVER A LAZY DOG.

MONUMENTALER MONOPOLIMONOLOG

Top left:
Narita Inspected book
foreword typed with
BD BDRmono font

Bottom:
«BD BDRmono»
Typedifferent font

www.typedifferent.com

Top Right:
«KD Kiste»
Monthly programme poster
420x420mm

Client:
Kulturhallen Dampzentrale,
Bern

1999

BD:104

Top:
«Sony Aibo»
Logotype proposal

Bottom:
«Awaiting bone posing»
3D Character design

Client:
Sony Robotics
Entertainment, Japan

2002

Unpublished

ALPHATRONIC

duke

«Alphatronic»
CD-sleeve
120x120mm

Client:
Daniel Wihler,
Inzec Records,
Bern

1999-2003

01 I deep in your soul   06:08
02 I slow slurp   06:36
03 I duke   08:06
04 I talk   06:07
05 I vocoman   06:18
06 I fluff fluff   06:02
07 I snake dream   05:51
08 I empty word   04:48
09 I solemn   05:00
10 I after 8 PM   08:04
11 I skip's heart   04:18
12 I big gray dog   04:20
13 I HAC   04:29

7 619969 999053

BD:106

«Auawirleben.00»
Theater programme
and poster
210X592mm
700X1000mm

Client:
Berner Ensemble

2000

auawirleben

Zeitgenössisches Theatertreffen in Bern
Kulturhallen Dampfzentrale • Schlachthaus Theater •
Tojo Reitschule • Kornhausbühne Stadttheater
25. Mai bis 10. Juni 2000

400 ASA (Zürich) • Sabine Harbeke (New York / Zürich) • Stadttheater Bern • Theaterhaus Jena •
Theater Basel • Hochschule für Musik und darstellende Kunst (Frankfurt a.M.) •
TIF Theater in der Fabrik (Dresden) • Menke / Kathir / Wigget (Zürich / Marseille) •
Panoptikum Pazzo (Bern) • Gendertainment (Basel)

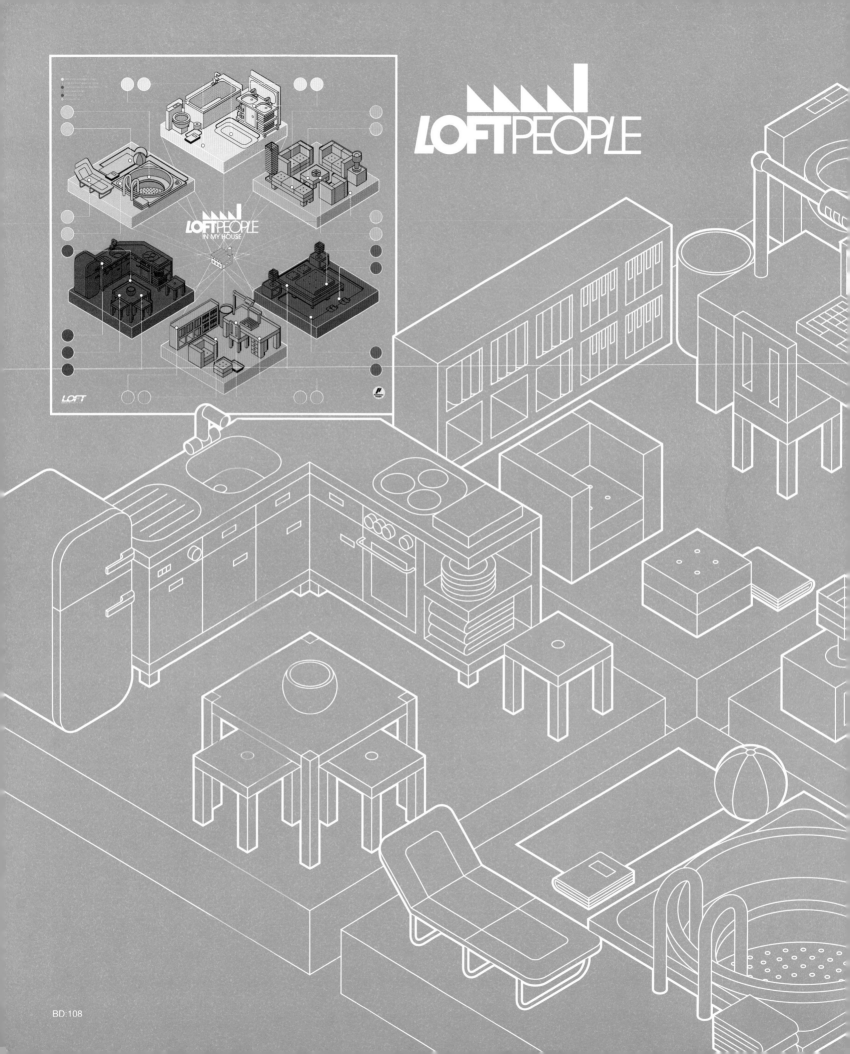

«Loftpeople»
Logotype, poster and flyers
420x420mm
140x140mm

Client:
British American Tobacco,
Parisienne/Loft Club,
Lausanne

2002

bla
bla bla
bla bla...

«Selected KD items»

Client:
Kulturhallen
Dampfzentrale,
Bern

2000-2002

Unpublished

KULTUR-
HALLEN
DAMPF-
ZENTRALE

foyer

BD:111

20000

«20000 Millenium Bug»
Monthly programme
poster
420x420mm

Client:
Kulturhallen
Dampfzentrale,
Bern

1999

10.-
ENTRÉE

10.- WIP

Top:
«Entry fee»
Hand drawn sign
for a Büro Discotec
in Geneva

2002

Unpublished

Bottom:
«Sweet&Sexy Vespa»
Illustration

Client:
Sweet&Sexy

2001

«Falling leafs
from Budapest»
Illustration

2002

www.lopetz.com

BD:115

guestbook entry

date: 2002-06-21 / 15:57:06
from: erolgemma
email:
erolgemma@hotmail.com
url: n/a
city: Lausanne
country: CH

PLEASE refresh your guest-
book... The Rest is PERFECT
Had a lot of fun «reading»
Narita.
I also like the work you did
for the Reithalle/BE

«Hôtel Des Deux Gares, Paris»
Büro Destruct Guestbook
Website

2000

www.burodestruct.net

guestbook entry

date: 2002-12-03 / 21:07:43
from: Jan Gjønnes Møller
email: gjonnes@paradis.dk
url: n/a
city: Copenhagen
country: Denmark

You should be able to piss a logo in the snow - you guys have a massive amount of urin. All in good taste...

Mind you – This is suppose to be a compliment.

Great respect.

guestbook entry

date: 2002-09-30 / 03:48:15
from: yuuta
email: otooto2002jp@yahoo.co.jp
url: www.goddog-pro.com
city: tokyo
country: sinjyuku

He wishes to be mostly touched by your design in my everyday life which is present in Japan!!!

«5x5<Pixler>»
Flash application

The 5x5<Pixler> shows
all 32'768 possible symmetric
symbols based on a 5x5
pixel grid.

Basic and flash encoding:
Michael Gianfreda

2000

www.burodestruct.net/
bd/bd5x5p/bd5x5p.html

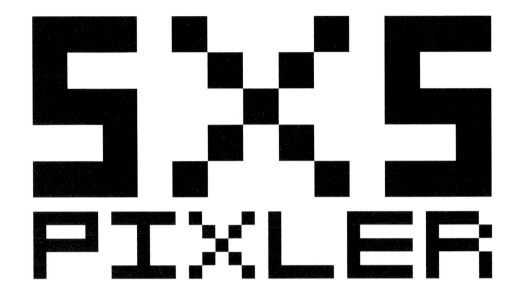

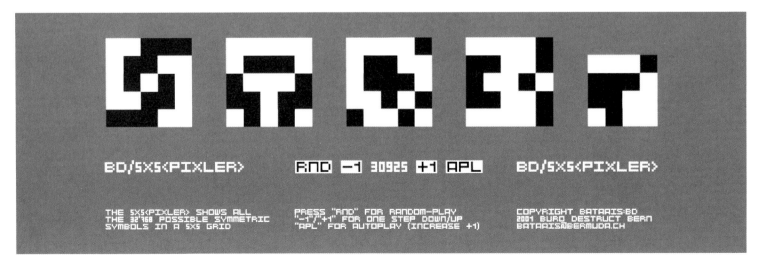

«Give Peas A Chance»
Compilation LP- and CD-
sleeve
313x313mm
121x121mm

Client:
Crippled Dick Hot Wax,
Berlin

2002

Top and right:
«Dormy»
Character design

Bottom:
«BD Orlando»
Typedifferent font

2002

www.typedifferent.com

bd orlando
abcdefghijklmnopqrstuvwxyz
abcdefghijklmnopqrstuvwxyz
0123456789
!"#¥€¥'/.&'()°+,-./:;<=>!@()¯_ˉ
äåòöüüæäâçéèêëïîìíøóôùúû
ßßç©¨«»☺

«Sweet&Sexy»
Flyers and posters
120x120mm, 420x420mm

Client:
Sweet&Sexy
2001-2002

Saturday, 4. May 02
at Temple, Berne
Open Doors: 22.00 h
Admission: 20 years

Dj's: Remady,
Player, Careem,
Tom Tronik &
Greg «Gee» Leone
MC's: Sharky-P (UK),
Tag Mc & Mc D-Fine

New Sweet&Sexy
CD 3 available!

Sweet&Sexy

Saturday,
5. January 2002
at Temple, Berne
Open Doors: 22.00 h
Admission 20 years

Djs: Player,
Remady,
The Grim Reaper,
Jamez, Source
Tag MC & D-Fine

Sweet&Sexy

Sweet&Sexy
UK House&Garage

Saturday, 10. Novembre 2001
at Temple, Berne
Open Doors: 22.00 h
Admission 20 years

Dj's: Ray Hurley (UK),
Remady, Player, Careem,
GrimReaper (Nasty Collective)
Mc D-Fine & Tag Mc

Saturday
1. Dezembre 2001
at Temple, Berne
Open Doors: 22.00 h
Admission 20 years

Dj's: Player,
Remady, Mark K,
Marc Blame, A. Lennix
MCs: CKP (UK)
& D-Fine

Sweet&Sex
UK House&Garage

Sweet&Sexy
CD-sleeve and poster
120x120mm
500x700mm

Client:
Sweet&Sexy

2002

Sweet&Sexy
Mixed by Player&Remady
«Booohh»

«Sweet&Sexy»
Flyer and poster
120x120mm
420x420mm

Client:
Sweet&Sexy

2002

BD:124

«Rasta»
Illustration

1991

www.lopetz.com

«Electronics Empire»
Exhibition poster
Nisen Tokyo
700x1000mm

Client:
Nisen/PGX, Japan

2000

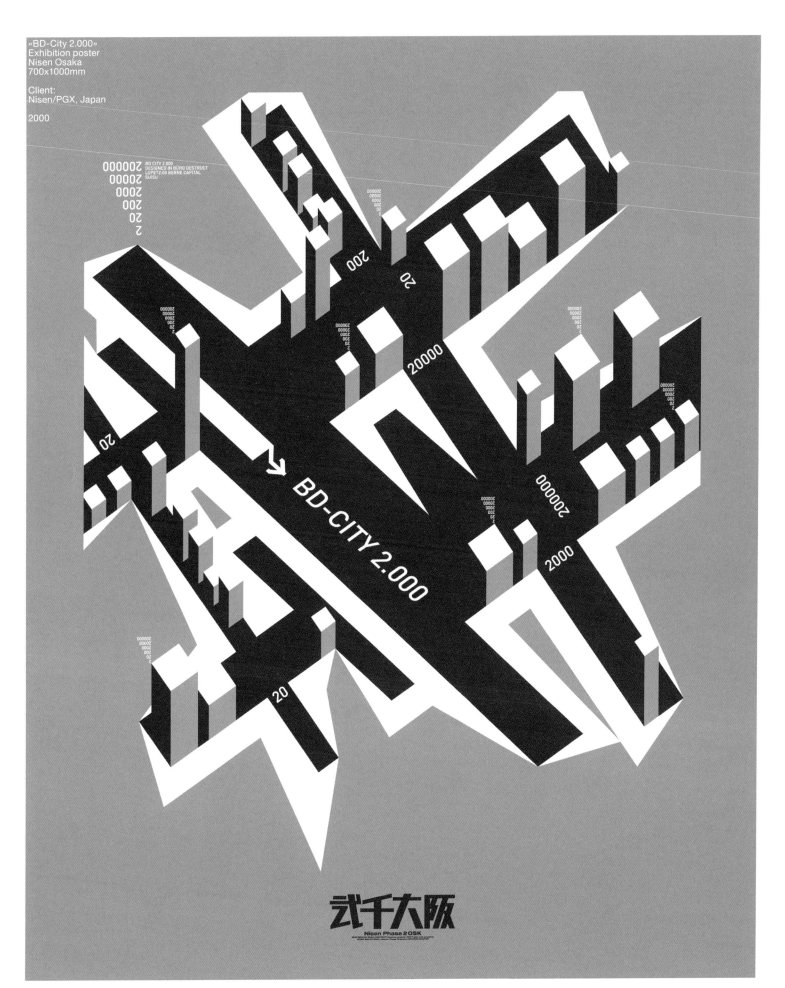

«BD-City 2.000»
Exhibition poster
Nisen Osaka
700x1000mm

Client:
Nisen/PGX, Japan

2000

«Olmo Stickers»

Client:
Olmo, Bern

2000-2002

Top:
«BD Ritmic»
Typedifferent font

2002

www.typedifferent.com

Bottom:
«Ritmic Swiss Tools»
EP-sleeve
313x313mm

Client:
Ritmic Records

2002

bd Ritmic

abcdefghijklmnoPqRstuuwXYz
abcdefghijklmnoPqRstuuwXYz
0123456789
(\)_'!"#+'()⬡+,-./:;<=>?@

KULTURHALLEN DAMPFZENTRALE   MBRUNNER BÜRO DESTRUCT 2002   SERIGRAPHIE ULDRY HINTERKAPPELEN

«Swiss Culture»
Monthly programme
poster

Client:
Kulturhallen
Dampfzentrale,
Bern

2000

Grounding Swiss Economy
= Swiss Culture

swiss culture

KINO in der Reitschule

EN ROUTE - AUS FRANKREICH

KINO in der Reitschule

MODIPOWER WOCHEN IM KINO

KINO in der Reitschule

STERNSTUNDEN DES KINOS

KINO in der Reitschule

SCIENCE & FICTION

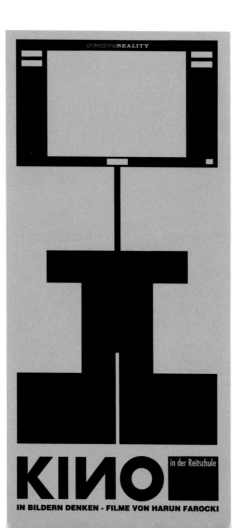

KINO in der Reitschule

IN BILDERN DENKEN - FILME VON HARUN FAROCKI

KINO in der Reitschule

BETTGESCHICHTEN IM KINO™

balduin
CHOOSE CHEESE

A
CHOOSE CHEESE 06:01
CHOOSE CHEESE REMIXED 03:54

B
CROQUE MONSIEUR 03:29
CROQUE MONSIEUR REMIXED 01:47

(C) 2002 CRIPPLED DICK HOT WAX! BERLIN-GERMANY
WWW.CRIPPLED.DE INFO@CRIPPLED.DE
PUBLISHED BY EDITION MONITORPOP / WARNER CHAPPELL
EFA 27619-6 • CDHW083 • MADE IN GERMANY
(LC 9759)

ALL MUSIC COMPOSED, PERFORMED & COOKED BY BALDUIN
AT CREATIVE COOKERY ROOFROOM 1999/2000.
THANKS TO MY BROTHERS LOPETZ & BATAAIS (KALEIDOPHONE),
KUSI (FOR USING SOME DRUM TAKES), MR HULOT & TOURISTS,
MY HOST PARENTS MR & MRS POTTS FROM ULCOMBE GARDENS,
SAINT PETER SCHOOL STUDENTS FROM CANTERBURY,
AND JUNKO FOR GIVING ME LOTS OF LOVE.
SLEEVED AT BÜRO DESTRUCT BERNE CAPITAL BY LOPETZ02.
SOURCE PHOTO: TONI IN KANDERSTEG
BALDUIN@BERMUDA.CH WWW.BERMUDA.CH/BALDUIN

Left page:
«Kino in der Reitschule»
Monthly cinema progamme
flyer
105x210mm

Client:
Kino in der Reitschule

2000-2003

Top:
«Balduin: Creative Cookery»
LP- and CD-Sleeve
313x313mm

Client:
Crippled Dick Hot Wax,
Berlin

2001

www.bermuda.ch/balduin

Bottom:
«Balduin: Choose Cheese»
Maxi sleeve
313x313mm

Client:
Crippled Dick Hot Wax,
Berlin

2002

www.bermuda.ch/balduin

«Sommerfoyer»
Logotype

«BD Balduin»
Typedifferent font

2001

www.typedifferent.com

Bottom:
«Sommerfoyer»
Programme flyer
630x148mm

Based on a photo by:
Claudio Vitale

Client:
Kulturhallen Dampfzentrale,
Bern

2002

Top:
«Plaid»
Concert poster and flyer
120x120mm
420x420mm

Client:
Reitschule, Bern

2001

Right:
From BD Balduin font
to Plaid poster

«BD Delafrance»
Typedifferent font

2000

www.typedifferent.com

BD DELAFRANCE
ABCDEFGHIJKLMNOPQRSTUVWXYZ
0123456789_L!"(+,-./:?=:;,ÄİÂÖÜ

«SF2LA»

1999

Unpublished

Top right:
«Wurst Case»

«BD Wurst»
Typedifferent font

2000

www.typedifferent.com

Drawings
on a «La Pizzeria»
restaurant table-set
during a büro discount
meeting

2003

Unpublished

BD WURST

"IN THE WORST CASE USE THE WURST"

ABCDEFGHIJKLMNOPQRSTUVWXYZ
0123456789ÄÖÜ¥«<>
[\]!""/&'()*+,-./:;<=>?@Q_`

BD:137

«Büro Discount»
Shop design

Graphics-Gallery-
Gimmicks-Gadgets

Zurlindenstrasse 226
8003 Zürich
Switzerland

2002

www.burodiscount.net

«Büro Discount»
Poster
700x1000mm

2002

www.burodiscount.net

büro™
discount

büro discount, graphics-gallery-gimmicks-gadgets, zurlindenstrasse 226, 8003 zurich, switzerland, phone: +41 (0)43 960 99 43, burodiscount@bermuda.ch www.burodiscount.net wednesday and friday 12:00-18:30, saturday 12:00-16:00

BD:139

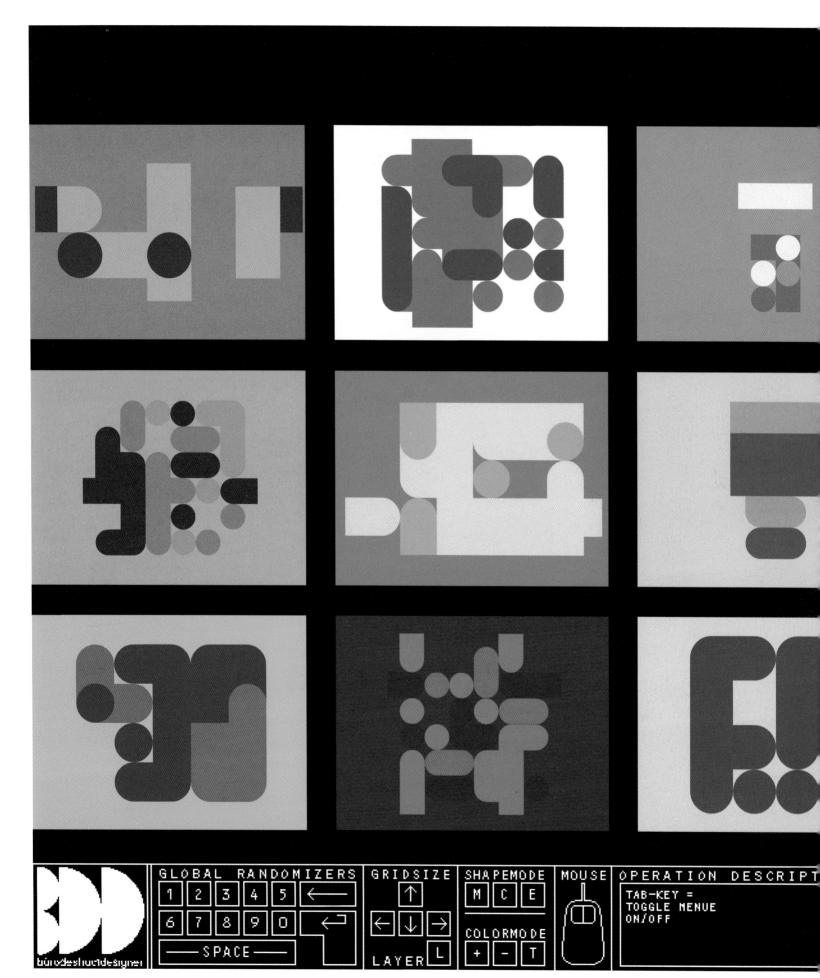

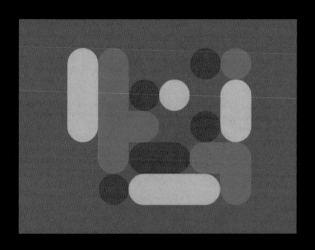
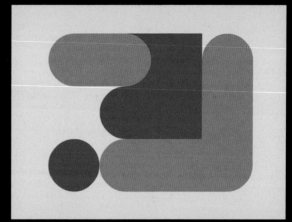

«BDD Designer»
Screenshots from the
BDD application and
screensaver

A tribute to the godfathers
of Swiss Graphic Design

Idea:
Michael Gianfreda
Programming:
Kaspar Lüthi, Humantools

1999

www.burodestruct.net/bd/
bddesigner/

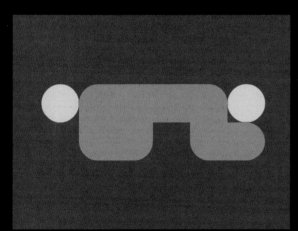
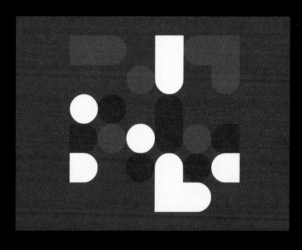

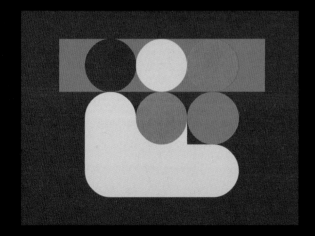
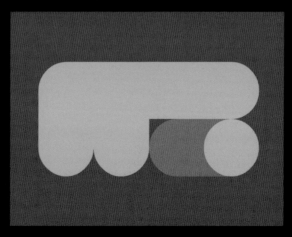

Bottom:
BDD Designer application
control unit

1999

www.burodestruct.net/bd/
bddesigner/

Left:
«Loslogos»
Logotype

2002

www.loslogos.org

Digitale Parallelstadt als Überlebensstrategie.

Wer hätte das gedacht: Das Internet emanzipiert sich von seinen Ideologen und führt mit einer gehörigen Portion Ironie die Visionen einer Esther Dyson, eines Nicolas Negroponte und des politischen Zentralorgans WIRED irgendwie ad absurdum. Zumindest in einem, die visuelle Kultur (oder Unkultur) der Global Economy und die Identität ihrer Player reflektierenden Bereich. Stichwort Logo.

Während nämlich die identitätsstiftenden Zeichen der Hochge-jubelten und Nasdaq-Lieblinge aus den Neunzigern gleich reihen-weise gnadenlos von den Festplatten gelöscht und aus dem Ver-zeichnissen von Google und Yahoo gestrichen werden, machen sich diejenigen der Totgesagten in der Realwelt schon fast Wegrationalisierten klammheimlich im Netz breit: Sie transzendieren in eine digitale Parallelstadt, die sich als Safe Heaven für Local Logos aus allen fünf Kontinenten etabliert hat.

Klar, dass eine solche Initiative nicht von den Betroffenen selbst ausgehen konnte: Der zwischen einem Starbuck-Stützpunkt und einem knalligen McDonald-Fresstempel eingeklemmte Teashop-Besitzer irgendwo in Shanghai oder Bejing hat weiss Gott andere Sorgen, als sein Logo in die Virtualität zu retten. Der aus realsozial-istischen Zeiten stammende Optikerladen in Rostock oder Leipzig, in dessen unmittelbarer Nachbarschaft plötzlich der Brillen-Fiel-mann seine Corporate Identity-Muskeln spielen lässt, ebenfalls. Und falls die Bauspekulanten und Immobilienhaie in einem latein-amerikanischen Megalopolis wieder mal ein neues Objekt ihrer Begierde in Gestalt eines pittoresken Quartiers entdecken und plattwalzen möchten, dann fürchten sich die kleinen Laden- und Barbesitzer nicht vor dem Verlust ihrer Logos, sondern vor dem Verlust ihrer wirtschaftlichen Existenz.

Die gefährdeten Logos brauchten also Überlebenshilfe von anderer Seite: von Leuten, die es schlicht und einfach nicht hinnehmen wollten, dass diese lokalen Identitätsstifter mit all ihrem Charme nach der verqueren Logik der Effizienz einfach so verschwinden müssen. Also haben sie die Gesellschaft zur Erhaltung des urbanen visuellen Erbes gegründet und eine digitale Logostadt im Netz eta-bliert: LosLogos.org. Bereits jetzt wird die Stadt von zahlreichen Logos bevölkert. Damit die Bevölkerungszahl weiter zunehmen kann, ist die Mithilfe von Gleichgesinnten gefragt: Wenn Sie also das nächste Mal mit ihrer Digikamera irgendwo auf der Welt unter-wegs sind, dann lichten Sie bitte nicht nur Ihre Lieblingsmotive ab, sondern halten auch Ausschau nach lokalen Logos, Ladenschildern und Schriftzügen – je skurriler und typischer, desto besser. Wie Sie Ihre Fundstücke ganz einfach in die digitale Stadt implementieren können, erfahren Sie auf der Website.

A digital parallel-city as survival strategy

Who would have thought: The Internet emancipates itself from its ideologists and with a healthy portion of irony leads the visions of Esther Dyson, Nicolas Negroponte and that of the central political organ WIRED somewhat to absurdity. This is particularly so, in the one area that reflects on the visual culture (or anti-culture) of the global economy and the identity of its players. The word logo is the cue.

At the same time, as the identity-symbols to the celebrated NAS-DAQ-darlings of the nineties, disappear en masse from hard disks and directories, the supposedly dead signs and symbols from the real world, sneakily grow in numbers on the internet. They tran-scend into a digital parallel city, which has established itself as a safe haven for local logos from all five continents.

Obviously, such an initiative could not have come from those affected directly: The owner of a tea parlour somewhere in Shang-hai or Beijing – squashed in between a Starbucks-base and a shiny McDonalds food-palace – by god has other things to worry about than saving his logo into virtual space. The same goes for the opti-cian in Rostock or Leipzig, who's shop dates back to communist times, as the multinational optician Fielmann flexes its corporate muscle in his immediate neighbourhood. If speculators and pro-perty tycoons in a Latin-American megalopolis set their eyes on a picturesque neighbourhood as their new object of desire (meaning they're dying to level the lot), the owners of small bars and shops won't be fearing for their logos, but for the very means of their existence.

To survive, the endangered logos needed help from a different side. Help from people, that were no longer willing, to let the symbols of local identity with all their charm, fall prey to the twisted logic of efficiency. So, these people founded the Society for the Conservation of Urban Visual Heritage and established a virtual logo-city on the Internet: LosLogos.org. This city is already inhabited by numerous logos. In order for its population to further grow, support is needed from likeminded people: Next time you travel anywhere in the world with a digital camera, please don't just photograph your favourite motifs, but also look out for local logos, shop signs and letters – the weirder and typical, the better. On the website you will see, how easy it is to integrate your find-ings into the digital city.

Text:
Roland Müller
Translation:
Kevin Mueller

Losologos.org, The Society
for the Conservation of
Urban Visual Heritage
founded and designed by
büro destruct.

With the participation of CUE
Institute of Contemporary
Urban Encounters.

Website coding:
Kaspar Lüthi, Humantools.

2002

www.loslogos.org

NAVIGATION HELP   KEYBOARD FUNCTIONS

**MOUSECLICK ON THE SHOCKWAVE WINDOW
TO ACTIVATE KEYBOARD COMMANDS**

N **N KEY =**
SWITCH WHITE/BLACK BACKGROUND

↑ ← ↓ → **ARROW KEYS =**
NAVIGATION DIRECTION

F / **C** **F KEY =** **C KEY =**
GO FAR / COME CLOSE

G / **V** **G KEY =** **V KEY =**
VIEW UP / VIEW DOWN

H / **B** **H KEY =** **B KEY =**
TARGET UP / TARGET DOWN

MOUSECLICK ON A LOGO TO ZOOM ONTO

Navigation help window

2002

www.loslogos.org

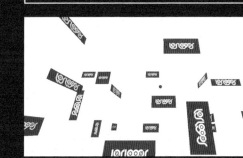

Screenshots of the site

2002

www.loslogos.org

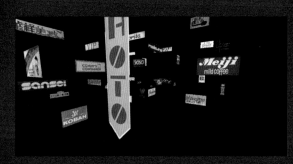

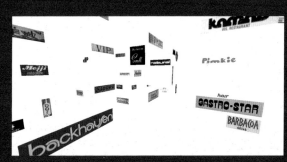

«Extra Terrestrial»
Monthly programme
poster
905x1280mm

Client:
Kulturhallen
Dampfzentrale,
Bern

2003

BD:145

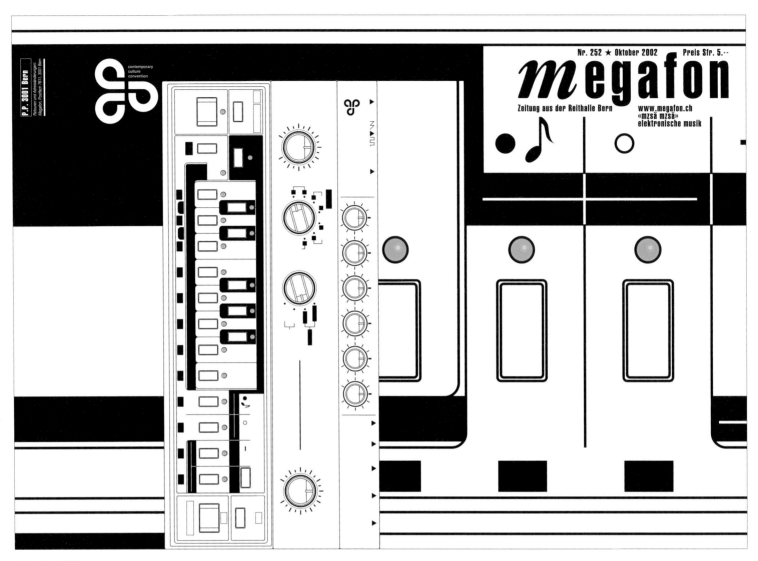

«Megafon #252»
Magazine cover
Topic: Electronic music
420x297mm

Client:
Reitschule, Bern

2002

Right page:
«BD AsciiMax»
«BD Zenith»
Typedifferent fonts

1999/2003

www.typedifferent.com

ABCDEFGHIJKLMN
OPQRSTUVWXYZ
1234567890.

«BD Breakbeat»
Typedifferent font

2003

www.typedifferent.com

BD Zenith
ABCDEFGIHJKLMNOPQRSTUVWXYZ
abcdefghijklmnopqrstuvwxyz
0123456789
■[/]!"#%'()*+.,:;-_\<=>?«»‹›←→°•—""''‹›bd TM
ÄäÖöÜüáâàéêè£ß¥€$S&℗☀®©

BD Ascii Max

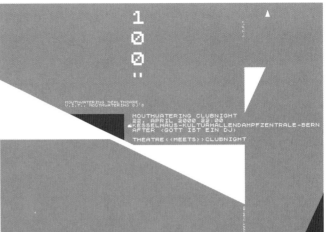

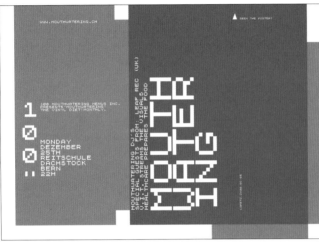
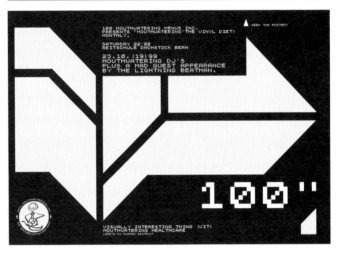

«Mouthwatering»
Clubnight flyers
148x105mm

Client:
Mouthwatering Inc,
Reitschule, Bern

1999-2002

www.mouthwatering.ch

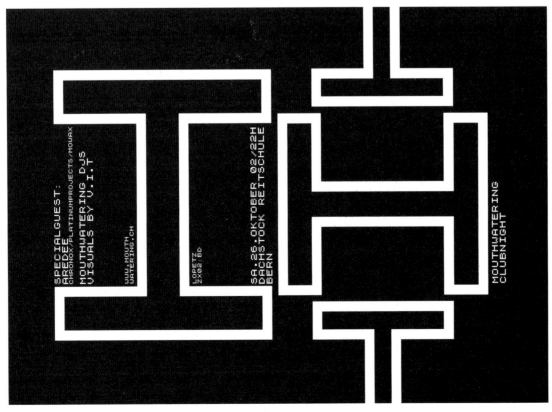
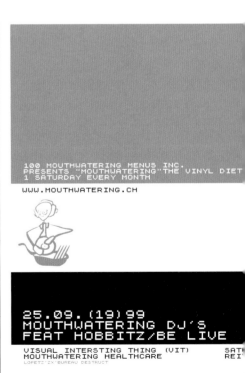

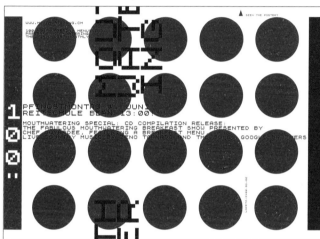

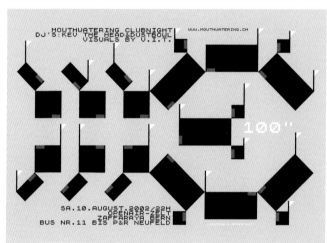

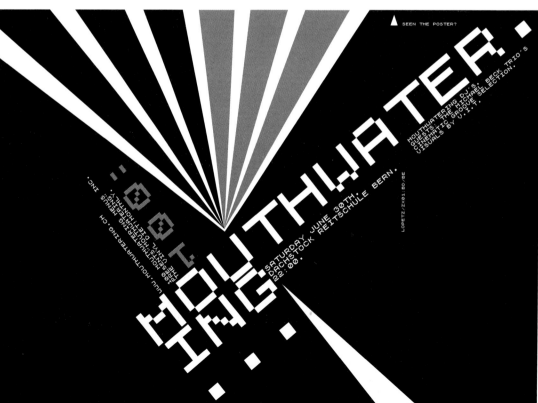

logofolio

Top left to bottom right: «Deka Dance», Client: Leila Benaissa, 2001 / «Aibo», Client: Sony Robotics Entertainment, 2000 / «KD-Capital Culture», Client: Kulturhallen Dampfzentrale Bern, 2000 / «Torx», Client: Luzi De Beaufort, 1999 / «KD Digital», Client: Kulturhallen Dampfzentrale Bern, 2002 / «Swiss Music Export», Client: Migros Kulturprozent, Pro Helvetia, 2002 / «Bundlebit», Client: Zera&Kev's Bed&Breakfast, 2002 / «Morris/Audio», Client: Stefan Riesen, 2000 / «The Wave», Client: Eskimo, 2002.

Left page, top left to bottom right: «Mr. Tape», Selfpromotion, 2000 / «Fieldreport», Client: CUE, Institute of Contemporary Urban Encounters, 2001 / «Top Fuel», Client: Top Fuel Entertainment, 2003 / «InterCityStream», Client: Laurence Desarzens, 2000 / «X Games 2000», Client: ISPN, America, 2000 / «Westcoast Imports», Client: Danny Schneider, 2003 / «Debeaufort», Client: Luzi De Beaufort, 2002 / «Ultraviolet», Client: Largeur.com, 2003 / «Kiff», Client: Kultur in der Futtermehl Fabrik, 2001 / «Olmo Sports», Client: Olmo, 2001 / «The Little Eagle», Selfpromotion, 1999 / «Garish» Client: Arnold Meyer, 2000 / «Hotel», Client: Hotel, 2000 / «Realizers», Client: Bruno Wolf, 2002 / «MiraSuiza», Client: Präsenz Schweiz, EDA, 2002. Right page, top left to bottom right: «Berne Beats», Selfpromotion, 2002 / «MTV-Video Music Award», Client: MTV America, 2001 / «Büro Destruct», Selfpromotion, 2002 / «Very Cherry», Client: Very Cherry Erotic Dancers, 2001 / «Olmo», Client: Olmo, 2002 / «Terminal M», Client: Monika Kruse, 2000 / «X-Ray», Client: Peter Zemp, 2001 / «Big Star», Client: Studio Achermann, 2000 / «Delan Records», Client: Raphael DeLan, 1999 / «East Touch», Client: East Touch Magazine, HongKong, 2002.

berne beats

BD

MTV VIDEO MUSIC AWARDS 01

büro destruct

Very-cherry
Exotic Dancers
BD

TERMINAL M

X-RAY
Consulting AG

BIG STAR ®

DELAN records

EAST TOUCH 366
東.TOUCH

«Sweet&Sexy»
Illustration for poster
and flyer
700x700mm
120x120mm

Client:
Sweet&Sexy

2000

Left page:
«Sweet&Sexy»
Illustration for poster, flyer
and CD-sleeve
700x1000mm
120x120mm

Client:
Sweet&Sexy

2002

Left page:
«Dr. O. Gerie»
3D Character design

Client: DMZ

2000-2001

Top:
«Hugo Loetscher»
Monthly programme
poster
700x1000mm

Client:
Kulturhallen
Dampfzentrale,
Bern

2001

Bottom:
«BD Aroma»
Typedifferent font

2003

www.typedifferent.com

Top left to bottom right:

«Tresor Night»
Clubnight flyer
120x120mm

Client:
UpTown, Bern

2000

«Renegade Hardware»
Concert poster and flyer
120x120mm

Client:
Reitschule, Bern

2001

«Drum'n'Bass In Da Face»
Clubnight flyer
120x120mm

Client:
UpTown, Bern

2000

«The Psychonauts»
Concert flyer
120x120mm

Client:
UpTown, Bern

2000

«Schaltkreis»
Clubnight flyer
120x120mm

Client:
Gaskessel, Bern

1999

«Drum'n'Bass In Da Face»
Clubnight flyer
120x120mm

Client:
UpTown, Bern

2001

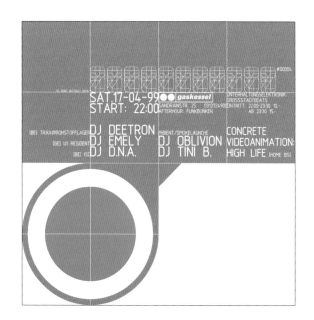

Top left to bottom right:

«Suv & Mc Tali»
Clubnight poster and flyer
420x420mm
120x120mm

Client:
Reitschule, Bern

2002

«Randall & Storm»
Clubnight poster and flyer
420x420mm
120x120mm

Client:
Reitschule, Bern

2000

«Kemal & Rob Data»
Clubnight poster and flyer
420x420mm
120x120mm

Client:
Reitschule, Bern

2001

«Full Cycle Night»
Clubnight poster and flyer
420x420mm
120x120mm

Client:
Reitschule, Bern

2001

«Audio Active»
Concert poster and flyer
420x420mm
120x120mm

Client:
Reitschule, Bern

2000

«Sylvester»
Sylvesterparty flyer
150x150mm

Client:
Kulturhallen
Dampfzentrale,
Bern

2000

«Barry»
Character design

Sketch for an
animation-movie

2001

™

BARRY™

バリー

«Jazz»
Illustrations for
BeJazz Winterfestival 2002
Poster, flyers and programme
booklet
420x420mm
148x105mm
120x120mm

Client:
Kulturhallen
Dampfzentrale,
Bern / BeJazz

2001-2002

BD:162

M. Branner

Young Pianist

Jimmy Smith

M. Branner

«Jazz Jam»
Illustration for
BeJazz Winterfestival 2002
Poster and programme
booklet
420x420mm
120x120mm

Client:
Kulturhallen
Dampfzentrale,
Bern / BeJazz

2001

BD:164

«Jazz Jam»
Illustration for
BeJazz Winterfestival 2003
Poster and programme
booklet
420x420mm
120x120mm

Client:
Kulturhallen
Dampfzentrale,
Bern / BeJazz

2002

 KULTURHALLEN
DAMPFZENTRALE

BEJAZZ

WINTERFESTIVAL 23.-26. JANUAR 2003

WWW.BEJAZZ.CH

DO 23.01. MENTOR NIGHT
FR 24.01. FUTURE NIGHT
SA 25.01. SATURDAY NIGHT
SO 26.01. FINAL NIGHT

VORVERKAUF: TICKETCORNER

«Dälek»
Concert poster and flyer
420x420mm
120x120mm

Client:
Reitschule,
Bern

2001

The posters image is made
out of this tiny JPG file
taken from the label's
website

150x50pixel/72dpi
4'072bytes

«Talvin Singh»
Logotag

Concert poster and flyer
420x420mm
120x120mm

Client:
Rote Fabrik,
Zürich

2000

«Dälek»
Concert poster and flyer
420x420mm
120x120mm

Client:
Reitschule,
Bern

2001

«Talvin Singh»
Logotag

Concert poster and flyer
420x420mm
120x120mm

Client:
Rote Fabrik,
Zürich

2000

«Danny Wheeler, Stamina Mc»
Logotag

Concert poster and flyers
420x420mm
120x120mm

Client:
Reitschule,
Bern

2002

LL building

ABCDEFGHIJKLMNOPQRSTUVWXYZ
abcdefghijklmnopqrstuvwxyz
1234567890(&.,!?;:)
§$%@*"/+-=

Left page:
«BD BillDings»
Typedifferent font

2002

www.typedifferent.com

«Type Robbery»
Akihabara, Japan
using Letterscan MC5

Speech for
Fresh Conference,
Singapore

2002

Unpublished

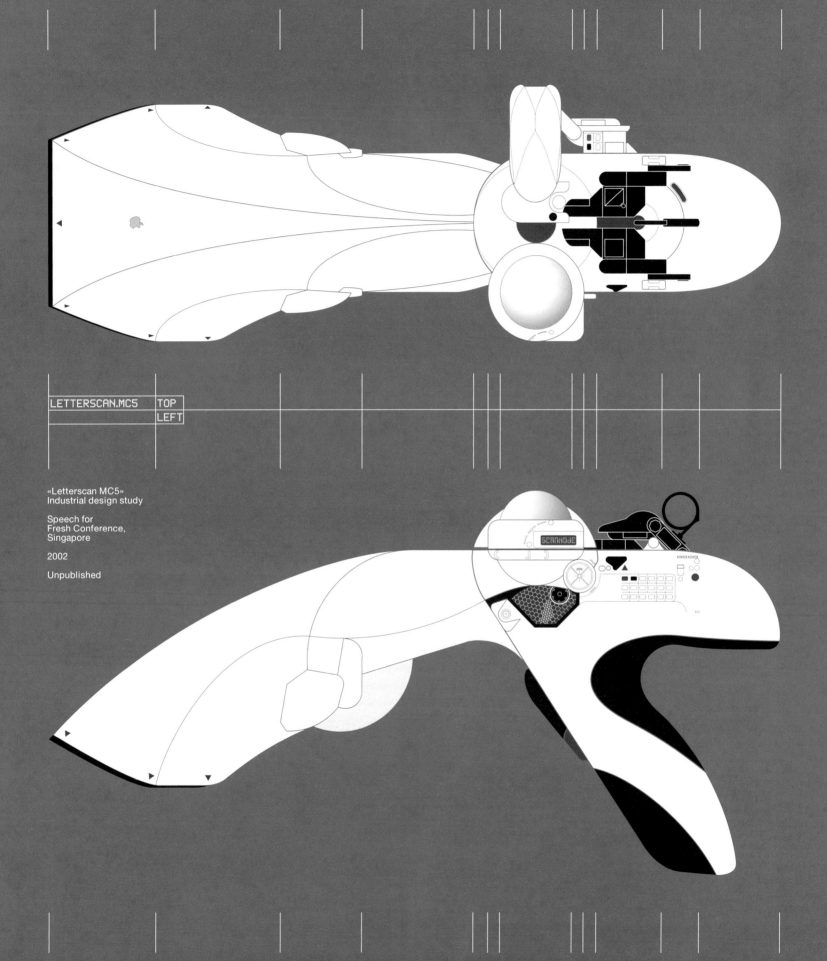

LETTERSCAN.MC5 | TOP
LEFT

«Letterscan MC5»
Industrial design study

Speech for
Fresh Conference,
Singapore

2002

Unpublished

Top:
«Electronic Plastic»
Book cover alternative version

Bottom:
Book cover final version

Page 174 and 175:
«Electronic Plastic»
Book spreads

ISBN# 3-931126-44-7

Published by
Die Gestalten Verlag, Berlin,
Jaro Gielens

2000

www.handhelden.com

www.burodestruct.net/bd/
etpbook/

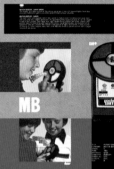

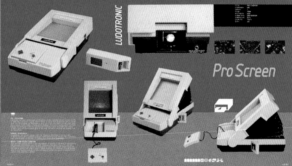

«Monkey Ass-Cards»
Joker playing cards
59x89mm

Client:
Parisienne,
British American Tobacco,
Lausanne

2002

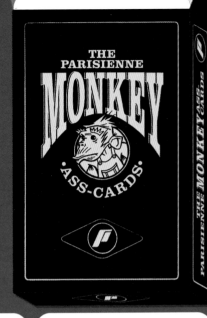

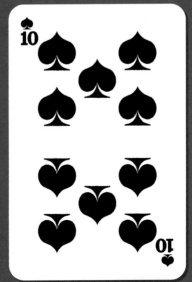

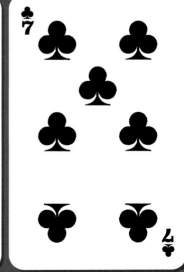

«Medifest.99»
Party poster
and flyer
297x420mm
210x148mm

Client:
Franz Martig

1999

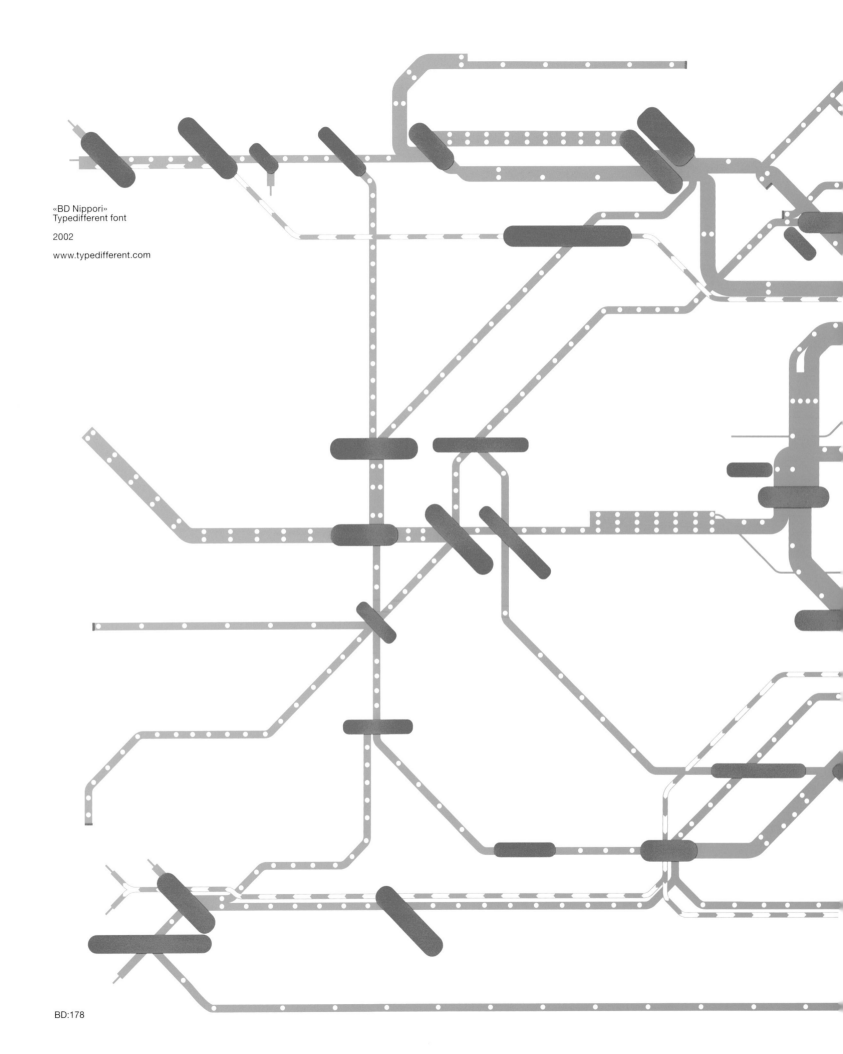

«BD Nippori»
Typedifferent font

2002

www.typedifferent.com

BD:178

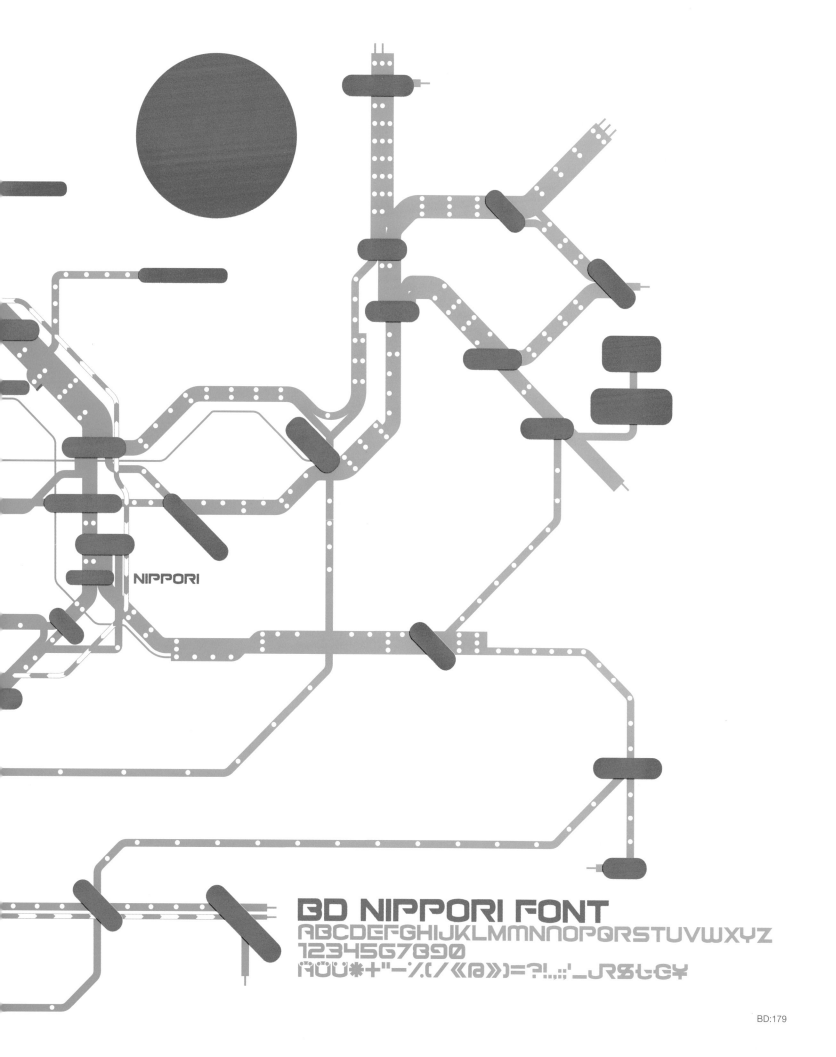

NIPPORI

BD NIPPORI FONT
ABCDEFGHIJKLMMNNOPQRSTUVWXYZ
1234567890
ÄÖÜ*+"-'.(/«ß»)=?!...:'_JR&bG¥

Left:
«Funkstörung»
Concert poster and flyer
420x420mm
120x120mm

Client:
Fri-Son, Fribourg

2002

Right:
«Lemon D & Dillinja»
Clubnight poster and flyer
420x420mm
120x120mm

Client:
Reitschule, Bern

2002

Bottom:
«MB»
Logotype

2001

Unpublished

Don't drink and drive

Schneider TM

Dj's: Feldermelder & Electric Sheep

Fri-Son Olive: Ma/Di 15.10.02/21h
Free Entry

«Schneider TM»
Concert poster and flyer
420x420mm
120x120mm

Client:
Fri-Son, Fribourg

2002

«Jura Pharmacy»
Flash animation
for splash site.

Sounds:
Balduin
www.bermuda.ch/balduin

Client:
Jura Apotheke,
Bern

2002

www.jurapharmacy.com

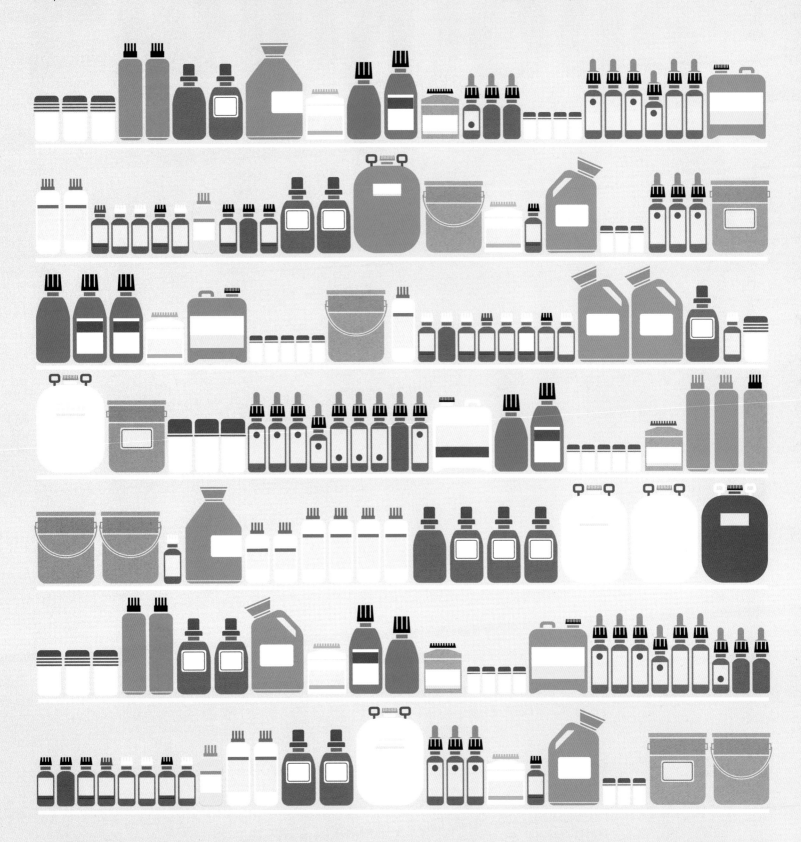

JURA APOTHEKE

M. KUBALA
BREITENRAINPLATZ 40
CH-3014 BERN

TEL   +41 (0)31 331 01 43
FAX   +41 (0)31 331 08 78
MAIL INFO@JURAPHARMACY.COM

DIE APOTHEKE   KONTAKT
DAS APO-TEAM MIRKO PRIVAT
ANGEBOTE   FREUNDE

apotheke✚

BD Apotheke

ABCDEFGHIJKLMNOPQRSTUVWXYZ
ÄÖÜÀÂÄÒÒÔÙÛÜÊÈÊ
abcdefghijklmnopqrstuvwxyz
äöüàâäòòôùûüêèê
1234567890=[{(«‹›»)}].,:;!?
©®ºß££$¥+"'*¡%&/@\‐–—_

«BD Apotheke»
Typedifferent font

2002

www.typedifferent.com

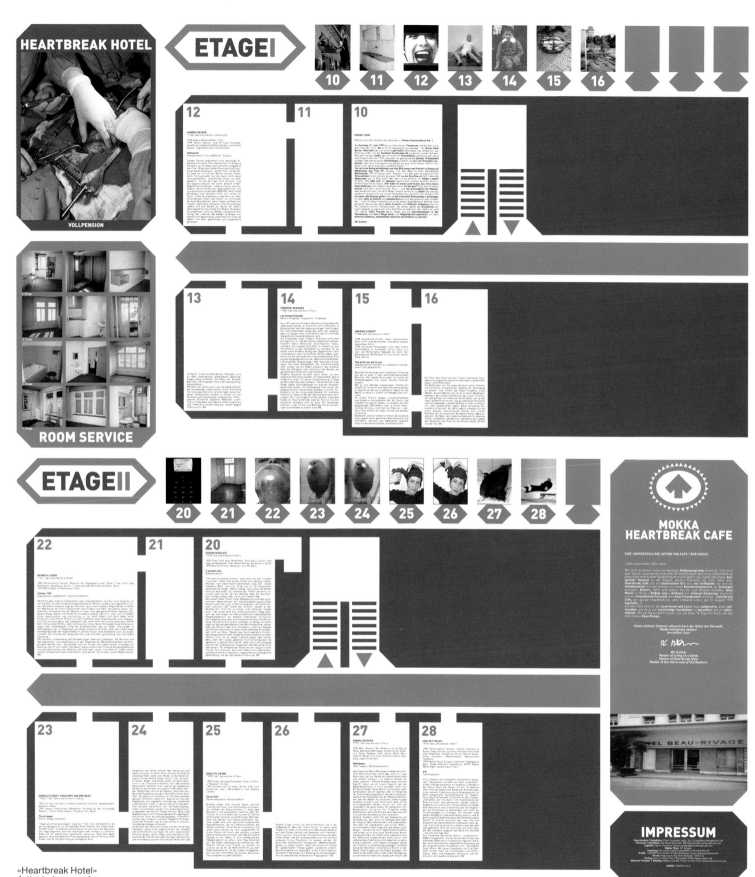

«Heartbreak Hotel»
Artist index map for
art exhibition in the ex-hotel
Beau-Rivage, Thun
840x740mm

Client:
Claire Schnyder Lüdi,
Bernhard Bischoff

1999

BERN TO BE INVADED

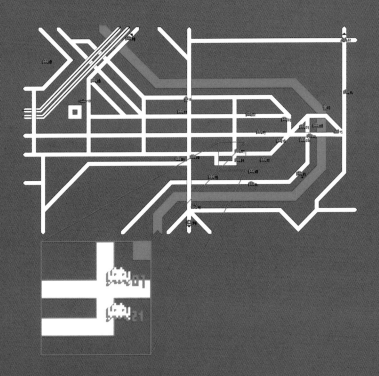

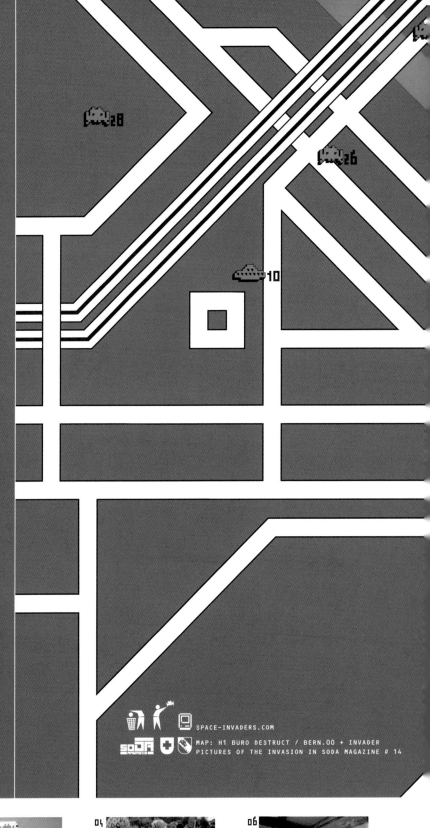

CARTE DE L'INVASION DE BERNE PAR SPACE INVADER.
DU 9 AU 16 MAI 2000.

MAP OF BERN INVASION BY SPACE INVADER.
9TH. TO MAY 16TH. 2000.

KARTE VON BERN INVASION DES SPACE INVADER.
09.05. BIS 16.05. 2000.

SPACE-INVADERS.COM

SPACE-INVADERS.COM

MAP: H1 BÜRO DESTRUCT / BERN.OO + INVADER
PICTURES OF THE INVASION IN SODA MAGAZINE # 14

Top:
«Bern To Be Invaded»
Space Invader Map
480x210mm

Bottom:
Location photos

Client:
Space Invader, Paris,
soDA Magazine

2000

www.space-invaders.com

Postgasse

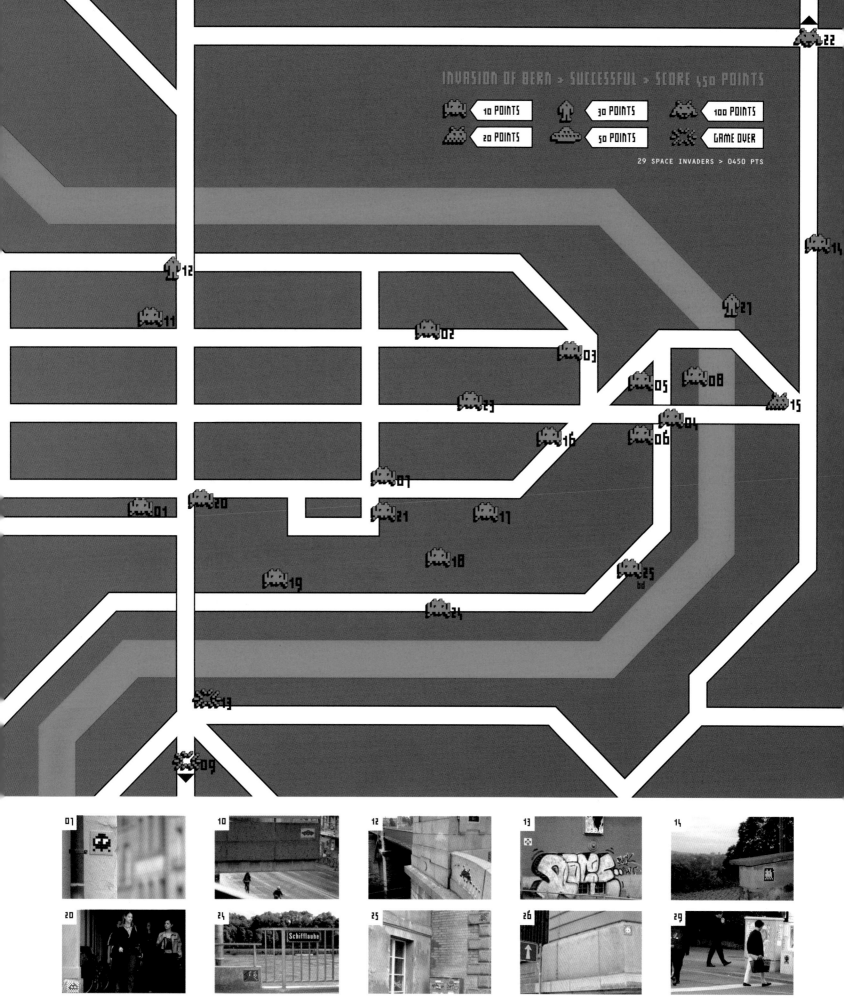

«Wizard»
Illustration

2001

www.lopetz.com

Right page:
«Tati: Playtime»
Flash animations
Bricollage with video stills.

Client:
Club Transmediale,
Berlin

2003

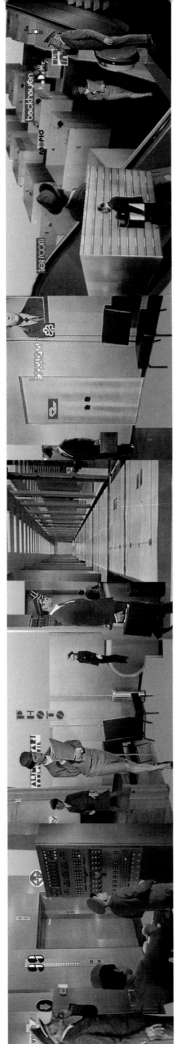

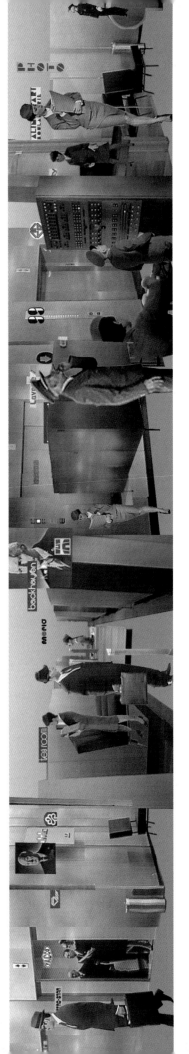

Top:
«Pipes & more»
Logotype

Bottom:
«Pipes & more»
Opening flyer
Front- and backside
148x105mm

Client:
Pipes and more,
Bern

2001

«Love May»
Monthly programme
poster
700x1000mm

Client:
Kulturhallen
Dampfzentrale,
Bern

2001

«Typedifferent.com»
Official büro destruct
font online shop

2002

www.typedifferent.com

typedifferent.com

PLAKATBAU — BD Plakatbau 1995
electrobazar — BD Electrobazar 1995
ELSIDE — BD Elside 1995
MEDLED — BD MedLed 1995
FLOSSY — BD Flossy 1995
PACCER — BD Paccer 1995
dippey — BD Dippex 1995
BROCKELMANN — BD Brockelmann 1995
RatterBit — BD RatterBit 1995
Faxer — BD Faxer 1995
Ticket — BD Ticket 1995
brick — BD Brick 1996
cluster — BD Cluster 1996
Fazer — BD Fazer 1996
Globus — BD Globus 1996
LODEL FIZLER — BD LodelFizler 1996
Rocket 70 — BD Rocket70 1996

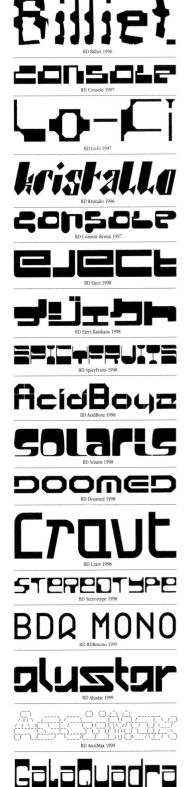

Billiet — BD Billiet 1996
console — BD Console 1997
Lo-Fi — BD Lo-Fi 1997
kristallo — BD Kristallo 1996
console — BD Console Remix 1997
eject — BD Eject 1998
eject katakana — BD Eject Katakana 1998
SPICYFRUITS — BD SpicyFruits 1998
AcidBoyz — BD AcidBoyz 1998
solaris — BD Solaris 1998
DOOMED — BD Doomed 1998
Cravt — BD Cravt 1998
STEREOTYPE — BD Stereotype 1998
BDR MONO — BD BDRmono 1999
alustar — BD Alustar 1999
AsciiMax — BD AsciiMax 1999
GalaQuadra — BD GalaQuadra 1999

Rainbow — BD Rainbow 2000
RELAUNCH — BD Relaunch 2000
Relaunch Katakana — BD Relaunch Katakana 2000
WURST — BD Wurst 2000
DELAFRANCE — BD DelaFrance 2000
colonius — BD Colonius 2001
Tatami — BD Tatami 2001
balduin — BD Balduin 2001
Mustang — BD Mustang 2001
bankwell — BD Bankwell 2001
billding — BD BillDing 2001
METER — BD Meter 2001
CashBox — BD CashBox 2001
Cash — BD Cash 2001
bd-ALM — BD Alm 2001

HexaDes — BD HexaDes 2001
CENTRAL — BD Central 2002
orlando — BD Orlando 2002
Apotheke — BD Apotheke 2002
BAND — BD Band 2002
BD-HELL — BD Hell 2002
Endless — BD Endless 2002
SweetHome — BD SweetHome 2002
Ritmic — BD Ritmic 2002
JURA — BD Jura 2002
NIPPORI — BD Nippori 2002
BONBON — BD BonBon 2002
AROMA — BD Aroma 2003
Zenith — BD Zenith 2003
NEBRASKA — BD Nebraska 2003

«Monsieur Poire»
Character design

Monsieur Poire is the
büro destruct spokesman

2000

Character
Sketches
1999-2003
Unpublished

FRITZ FERTIG

1000K.
1MB
1000MB
1GB
60GB
60'000MB

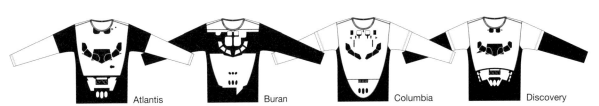

Atlantis   Buran   Columbia   Discovery

«Shuttle-Shirts»
XS, S, M, L

Photo: Regula Roost, Bern
Makeup: Anja Wiegmann,
Bern

Client:
∏a / Pia Affolter, Zürich

2002

MAS YENDO

IRONIC DIVERSION

アイロニック　ディバージョン

RIEA europa   Research Institute for Experimenal Architecture

Springer WienNewYork

«Ironic Diversion»
Cover and book design
180x210mm,
104 Pages

Client:
RIEAeuropa
Mas Yendo, New York

Editor:
Lebbeus Woods,
New York

Published by:
Springer Verlag
Wien/New York

ISBN 3-211-83492-3

2000

Page 198 and 199:
«Ironic Diversion»
Book spreads
360x210mm

Page 200:
«Ironic Diversion»
Icon collection

2000

Unpublished

UD-9010
UD-S.P.I.A プロジェクト.07
PROJECT.07

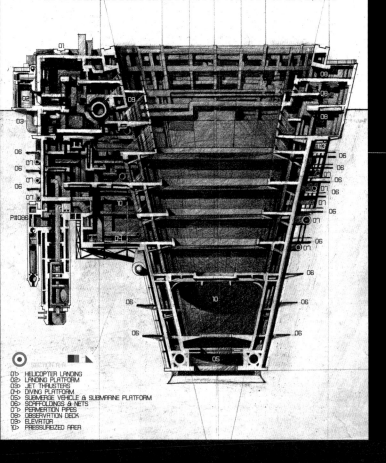

P#086

SECTION A-A

01> HELICOPTER LANDING
02> LANDING PLATFORM
03> JET THRUSTERS
04> DIVING PLATFORM
05> SUBMERGE VEHICLE & SUBMARINE PLATFORM
06> SCAFFOLDINGS & NETS
07> PERMEATION PIPES
08> OBSERVATION DECK
09> ELEVATOR
10> PRESSUREIZED AREA

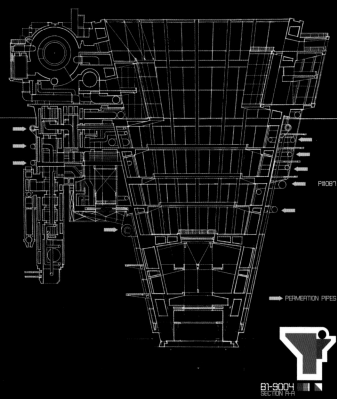

P#087

➤ PERMEATION PIPES

B1-9004
SECTION A-A

MANHATTAN

P#092

TITLE: UD-9601 PETROSINO PARK: THE INCISION
YEAR: SEPTEMBER, 1996
SITE: LAFAYETTE AND DELANCY STREET, PETROSINO PARK, NEW YORK, NY
PROGRAM: OUTDOOR PARK
DIMENSIONS: 6,400 SQ./FT.
COMPLETION: NOT BUILT

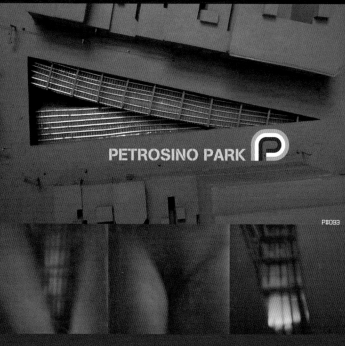

PETROSINO PARK

P#093

PETROSINO PARK/REDEVELOPMENT DESIGN COMPETITION
MANHATTAN HIGH-KU

A gray cloud hangs low in the sky, reflecting noise and trapping air.
Incandescent lamps cast shadows upward toward the buildings.
A silhouette appears against the headlights of speeding traffic.
Rivets protrude from steel beams; asphalt glistens like latex.
Steam erupts from manholes as pipes spurt noise onto the pavement above.
Sensuous curves of steel descend into the abyss.

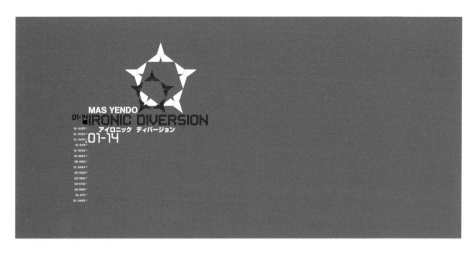

MAS YENDO
IRONIC DIVERSION
アイロニック ディバージョン
01-14

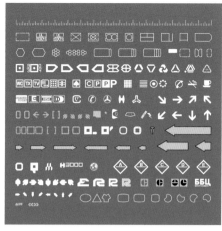

AUL-9205
UL-U.S.O.
UL-U.S.O.
UL-U.S.O.
A B C D E
UL-9205 プロジェクト.01
PROJECT.01
35085

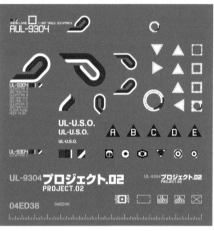

AUL-9304
UL-U.S.O.
UL-U.S.O.
UL-U.S.O.
A B C D E
UL-9304 プロジェクト.02
PROJECT.02
04ED38

AUL-B45
UL-U.M.O.
UL-U.M.O.
UL-U.M.O.
A B C D E
UL-B45 プロジェクト.04
PROJECT.04
25382GN

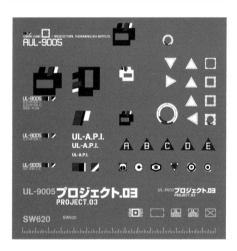

AUL-9005
UL-A.P.I.
UL-A.P.I.
UL-A.P.I.
A B C D E
UL-9005 プロジェクト.03
PROJECT.03
SW620

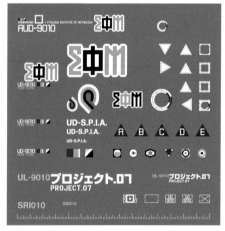

AUD-9010
UD-S.P.I.A.
UD-S.P.I.A.
UD-S.P.I.A.
A B C D E
UL-9010 プロジェクト.07
PROJECT.07
SRI010

AUL-9502
UL-M.O.M.A.
UL-M.O.M.A.
UL-M.O.M.A.
A B C D E
UL-9502 プロジェクト.05
PROJECT.05
M.O.M.A.

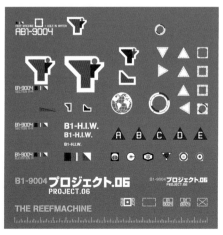

AB1-9004
B1-H.I.W.
B1-H.I.W.
B1-H.I.W.
A B C D E
B1-9004 プロジェクト.06
PROJECT.06
THE REEFMACHINE

AUD-9601
UD-T.I.
UD-T.I.
UD-T.I.
A B C D E
UD-9601 プロジェクト.10
PROJECT.10
PETROSINO PARK

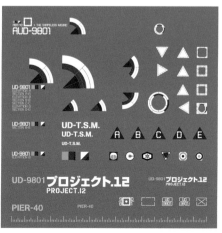

AUD-9801
UD-T.S.M.
UD-T.S.M.
UD-T.S.M.
A B C D E
UD-9801 プロジェクト.12
PROJECT.12
PIER-40

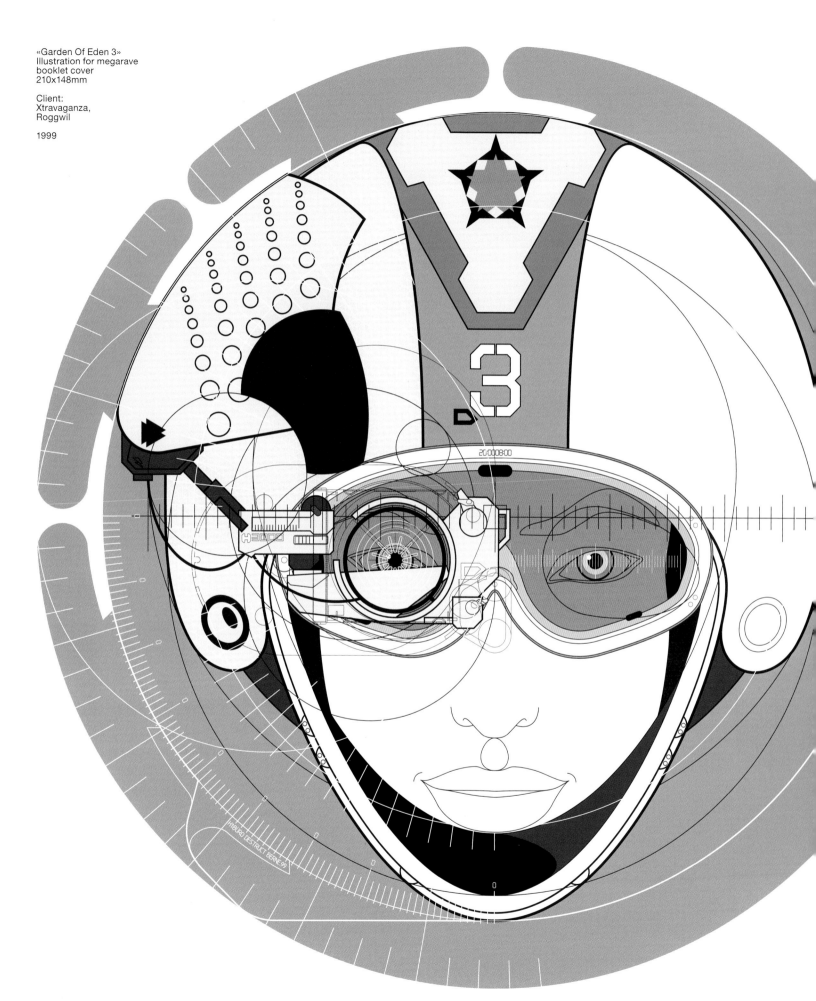

«Garden Of Eden 3»
Illustration for megarave
booklet cover
210x148mm

Client:
Xtravaganza,
Roggwil

1999

«Garden Of Eden 3»
Illustrations for megarave
booklet spreads
420x148mm

Client:
Xtravaganza,
Roggwil

1999

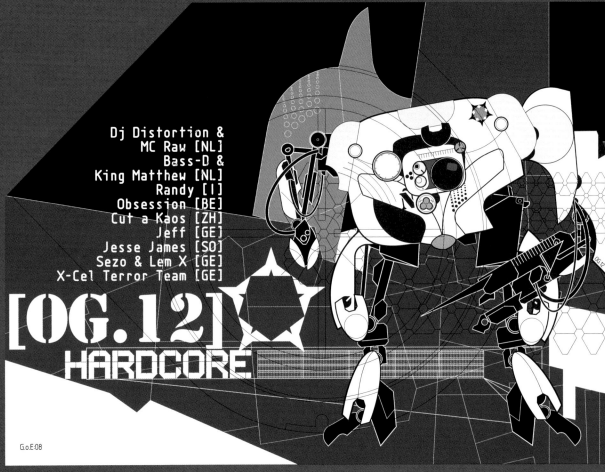

Dj Distortion &
MC Raw [NL]
Bass-D &
King Matthew [NL]
Randy [I]
Obsession [BE]
Cut a Kaos [ZH]
Jeff [GE]
Jesse James [SO]
Sezo & Lem X [GE]
X-Cel Terror Team [GE]

[OG.12]

HARDCORE

G.o.E:08

[UG.12]

Skaos [BE]
Dynamic [BE]
Fallovie [VS]
Nitro [AG]
Foxx [BE]
Mr. AL [GE]
Phrentic [ZH]
Max B Grant [ZH]
Betty Boop [BE]
Ryan Hawkin [BE]
Truce [BE]
Dave 202 [ZH]

HARDHOUSE-
CLUBTRANCE

G.o.E:10

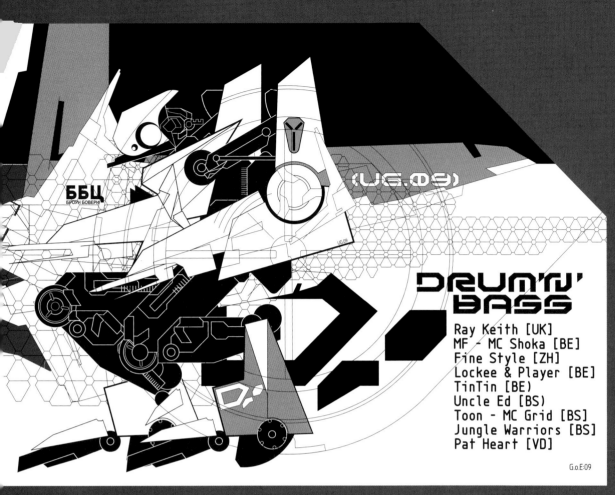

ББЦ
БРОУН БОВЕРИ

(UG.09)

DRUM'N' BASS

Ray Keith [UK]
MF - MC Shoka [BE]
Fine Style [ZH]
Lockee & Player [BE]
TinTin [BE]
Uncle Ed [BS]
Toon - MC Grid [BS]
Jungle Warriors [BS]
Pat Heart [VD]

G.o.E:09

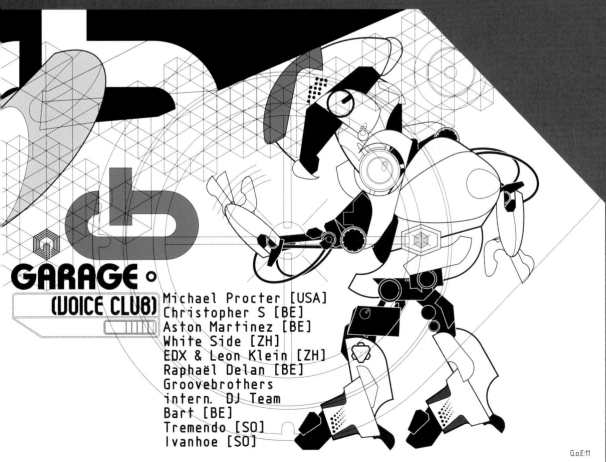

GARAGE °
(VOICE CLUB)

Michael Procter [USA]
Christopher S [BE]
Aston Martinez [BE]
White Side [ZH]
EDX & Leon Klein [ZH]
Raphaël Delan [BE]
Groovebrothers
intern. DJ Team
Bart [BE]
Tremendo [SO]
Ivanhoe [SO]

G.o.E:11

«Garden Of Eden 3»
Illustrations for megarave
booklet spreads
210x148mm

Client:
Xtravaganza,
Roggwil

1999

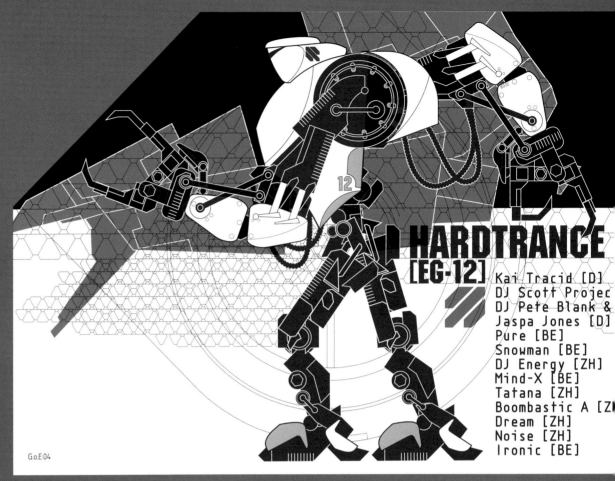

HARDTRANCE
[EG-12]

Kai Tracid [D]
DJ Scott Projec
DJ Pete Blank &
Jaspa Jones [D]
Pure [BE]
Snowman [BE]
DJ Energy [ZH]
Mind-X [BE]
Tatana [ZH]
Boombastic A [Z
Dream [ZH]
Noise [ZH]
Ironic [BE]

G.o.E:04

dETROIT
ELEKTRO
0609

K Hand [UK]
Darren Price [UK]
DMC David [ZH]
Lukas [TI]
Dee Tree 9 [BE]
Deetron [BE]
Willow [VD]
Jeff Swing [GE]
Dub [BE]
Weldon [GE]

G.o.E:06

EG.05

FLASH BACK

Placid Angel [ZH]
Dream [ZH]
Simple [ZH]
Lukas [TI]
Jumpin' Jack [ZH]
Noise [ZH]

G.o.E:05

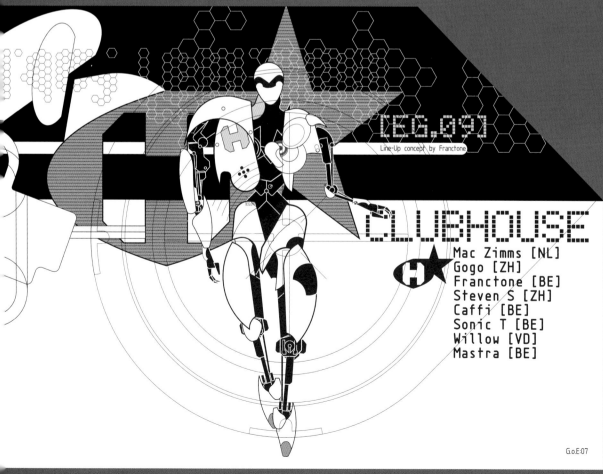

[EG.09]

Line-Up concept by Franctone

CLUBHOUSE

Mac Zimms [NL]
Gogo [ZH]
Franctone [BE]
Steven S [ZH]
Caffi [BE]
Sonic T [BE]
Willow [VD]
Mastra [BE]

G.o.E:07

Top left and right:
«V.I.D.»
Poster and postcard
for video-art festival
700x1000mm
105x148mm

Client:
V.I.D., Kulturhallen
Dampfzentrale,
Bern

2001

Bottom:
«V.I.D Video Award»
Logotype and animation
«RGB»
Character animation

Client:
V.I.D., Kulturhallen
Dampfzentrale,
Bern

2001-2002

V.I.D. BERN 2002
FESTIVAL FÜR VIDEOKUNST
5.–7. SEPTEMBER 2002

KULTURHALLEN
DAMPFZENTRALE BERN

«V.I.D. - RGB»
Festival for video-art
poster and video-award
character design
700x1000mm

Client:
V.I.D., Kulturhallen
Dampfzentrale,
Bern

2002

RGB

SoDA

#15

4/2000
ISLE OF JURA
(SCO)

SFR   8.-
DM   10.-
FF   35.-
$ 4.99
£   3.50

BURO
DESTRUCT

«Isle Of Jura»
Magazine cover
soDA #15
Cover for the photo
report about the Isle
of Jura.

Client:
soDA Magazine

2000

www.soda.ch

8 07297 00132 7

Í LOVE JURA

«Isle Of Jura – I Love Jura»
Logotype

2000

Angekommen in Ozeanien oder Eurasien. Innere Hebriden Schottland oder genauer Isle of Jura. Wir haben ein Tief und trinken billigen Whisky. Es hat geschneit in Schottland und damit haben wir nicht gerechnet. Wir fragen uns nach unseren Prinzipien und denken einen Moment nach. Was haben wir in Schottland verloren? Was ist unser Zweck? Wollen wir möglichst viele Menschen kennen lernen, um die Welt zu begreifen oder suchen wir nach dem Schönen in seiner natürlichen Umgebung? Die Isle of Jura ist eigentlich sowas wie ein Zweihundert-Seelen-Dorf. Das einzige, was diese Insel erlebt hat seit Hannibal die Alpen überquerte, ist, dass George Orwell hier sein Buch «1984» schrieb. Die Einheimischen leben vom Fischfang und von der Rotwildjagd. Und natürlich vom Whisky und einigen verirrten Touristen wie wir es zu sein scheinen. Doch suchen wir hier auch irgendwie ein Stück Heimat. Wenn ich von einer Suche spreche, wird das unserer Situation, unserer Idee, sozusagen unserem Plan, auch nicht in jeder Hinsicht gerecht. Es handelt sich dabei mehr um ein Herumlungern, kurzum: um ein Weiterkommen im erweiterten Sinn. Das Frühstück besteht hier einerseits aus einem Haufen Mehl und Ei und andererseits aus leicht blutigem Fleisch. Dann ist da noch dieser Mann. So ein alter Schotte. Er erzählt uns die Schauergeschichten von den sieben blutigen Köpfen, dem Fluch der Witwe und den bösen Feen von Craighouse. Alles gefährlich wie Curry-Sauce. Mit diesem irgendwie zwiespältigen Hintergrund kommen wir zu einem Schloss in einer Moorlandschaft. Am Wegrand ein Auto-Skelett. Das Schloss hat natürlich ein sehr eigenartiges Innenleben. Derart mysteriös, dass wir uns fragen müssen, was dieses Volk kulturhistorisch geleistet hat, ausser dass die Männer dämliche Röcke tragen und auf dem Dudelsack stupide Liebeslieder spielen. Eine gute Frage. Nun, die Kelten haben zumindest zwei Dinge erfunden, ohne die das Leben auf dieser Welt nicht ohne weiteres lebenswert wäre: die Seife und den Whisky. Gegen zwei Uhr ist endgültig ein Ausflug ins Grüne angesagt. Unsere nächste Station ist Sound of Jura. Wir stehen am Ufer und gucken rüber zum schottischen Highland. Zwar sieht man von unserem Standort aus das Highland gar nicht, aber das ist ein Detail. Die fünfte Whiskyflasche war einmal und es wird allmählich Zeit ein Pub aufzusuchen. Wir treten die Rückfahrt zum Hotel an. Immer wieder halten wir an um Fotos zu schiessen. In einer Schafsherde finden wir uns wieder. Von allen Tieren der Schöpfung ist das Schaf unbestritten eines der friedlichsten und gutmütigsten. Nur wenige Tiere – allenfalls die gemeine Hauskatze – machen einen ähnlich friedfertigen Eindruck. Von der Kälte müde, gehen wir in das erstbeste Restaurant. Das Restaurant «No Doubt». Jeder bestellt ein Bier und wir essen Seelachs mit Kartoffeln. Das Abendessen deckt vor allem den familiären Aspekt unserer Reise ab. Wir lernen einander besser kennen: «Wir versuchen ja irgendwie die ganze Sache zu kontrollieren.» «Das verstehe ich nicht. Was heisst da Kontrolle? Es geht eigentlich vor allem um Humor, nicht um den plumpen Witz als solches – es geht mehr um den Moment, wo das Lachen verstummt, der Moment, wo eine liebliche Grausamkeit beginnt.» «Und es geht um das Leben. Um das Füreinander und nicht um das Gegeneinander.» Demzufolge krebsen wir ins Hotelzimmer zurück und machen mit der Arbeit vorwärts. Dazu unseren eigenen Sound of Jura. Steil. Die Nacht heute gleicht ein bisschen der Nacht vom 20. März 1977. Oder der Nacht, vom 24. September 1978. Oder vielleicht auch einigen Novembernächten. Kein Blickdelikt mehr! Kein Wortdelikt mehr! Kein Gedankendelikt mehr! Keine Kontrolle mehr! Zimmer 101, Hotel Boldfont, I love Jura (kleines Wortspiel). Kapiert? Nicht kapiert? Auch gut.

Arrival in Oceania or Eurasia. Inner Hebrides, Scotland – Isle of Jura to be more precise. We're on a low, drinking cheap whiskey. It's been snowing in Scotland and we didn't expect that. We try to recall our principals and briefly consider our situation. What business have we in Scotland? What is our purpose? Is it that we want to get to know as many people as possible as to better understand the world or are we in search of beauty in its natural environment? The Isle of Jura in a way is like a village of two hundred odd souls. The only memorable thing happening on this island since Hannibal crossed the Alps, was that George Orwell came here to write his book "1984". The locals make a living from fishing, Deer-hunting, Whisky and a few lost tourists, -lost as we appear to them. It happens to be, that we're searching for a piece of home also. Speaking of a search doesn't quite describe our situation, our idea, our plan so to speak, – doesn't take into account every aspect. With us it's more of a lingering situation, - to put it briefly: getting on in an ongoing sense. Breakfast here consists of a heap of flour, eggs and slightly bloody meat. There is also this man. An old Scot. He tells us the gruesome story of the seven bloody heads, the curse of the widow and the wicked fairies of Craighouse. All dangerous like curry sauce. With somewhat dodgy background we arrive at a castle in a moor. The skeleton of a car at the wayside. Inside, the castle of course is very strange. So mysterious in fact, that we have to ask ourselves, what the people of Scotland have achieved historically, besides inventing skirts for men and playing dumb love songs on bagpipes. A good question. Well, the Celts have invented two things at least, without which life would not be quite so worthwhile: soap and whisky. Alas, towards two o' clock we're heading for a walk in the outdoors. Our next destination is sound of Jura. We stand on the shore and gaze over the water to the Scottish highland. We cannot actually see the highland from here but that's a negligible detail. The fifth bottle of whisky has long gone and it's getting time to head for the pub. We start heading back to the hotel. We keep stopping to take pictures. We find ourselves in herd of sheep. Of all animals created, the sheep is doubtless the most peaceful and benign creature. Only few animals – possibly the cat – give a similarly calm impression. Tired from the cold, we head for the first restaurant we come across. It is the restaurant «No Doubt». Each of us orders a beer and we eat Atlantic salmon with potatoes. The meal primarily covers the «family» aspect of our journey. We get to know each other more closely: «It is so, that we try to somehow keep control of the whole affair.» «This I don't understand. What might you mean by control? It is actually about humour first and foremost, not the clumsy joke as such – it is more about the point when laughter dies, the point where sweet cruelty begins.» «And it is about life. About being for one another and not against one another.» Subsequently we retreat to the hotel room to further advance our work. Our own sound of Jura playing. Steep. This night resembles the night of the 20th March 1977 a little. Or the night of 24th September 1978. Possibly also several November nights. More offence of the eye! No more offence of the word! No more offence of the mind! No more control! Room 101, Boldfont Hotel, I love Jura (small wordplay). Got it? Didn't get it? Just as well.

Photo-report text
(short version)
by HGB Fideljus

Translation
by Kevin Mueller

«Isle Of Jura»
Photo-report
Magazine spreads
soDA #15

Client:
soDA Magazine

2000

www.soda.ch

«Isle Of Jura»
Photo-report
Magazine spreads
soDA #15

Client:
soDA Magazine

2000

www.soda.ch

9 o'clock

Howard Jones

«Isle Of Jura»
Photo report
Magazine spreads
soDA #15

Client:
soDA Magazine

2000

www.soda.ch

«Isle Of Jura»
Photo-report
Magazine spreads
soDA #15

Client:
soDA Magazine

2000

www.soda.ch

restaurant
no doubt

Die Legende der Isle of Jura

Im Jahr 2000 bereisten wir, mit Blick auf unsere Titelstory im Schweizer Grafikmagazin Soda, die Isle of Jura bei Schottland, um nach Überresten der verbrannten Dollarmillion der Musikgruppe KLF zu suchen und eine sinnlose Menge schottischen Whisky zu trinken. In Wirklichkeit liessen wir die Chefredaktion und die Leserschaft des Magazins jedoch in eine Medienfalle tappen: Wir fuhren nur wenige Kilometer von unserem Wohnort entfernt, in den angrenzenden Berner Jura und kreierten Bilder und einen Begleittext, die durchaus in unserem offiziellen Reiseziel hätten entstehen können. Es ging uns darum, auf spielerische Weise zu demonstrieren, wie wenig es braucht, um visuelle Eindrücke und damit nicht zuletzt auch die Meinungsbildung zu manipulieren.

Isle of Jura Liner note

In the year 2000 we travelled to the Scottish Isle of Jura, with an upcoming cover story for the Swiss graphics magazine Soda in mind. We took the trip to the Isle of Jura in search of the remainders of the million dollars burnt by the music group KLF and to drink ridiculous amounts of Scottish whisky. In reality we led the editors and the readers of the magazine into a media-trap: We only travelled a few kilometres from where we live to the nearby Bernese Jura, creating images and a text that could just as well have been from our official destination. Our intention was to demonstrate in a playful way, how little it takes to manipulate visual impressions and also opinion-building for that matter.

Right:
The key
to the restaurant/hotel
«Du Doubs»

bd jura

abcdefghijklmnopqrdtuvwxyz
1234567890 («#&¿?'!*%.,;:–/>+=°»bd_)
äöüâáàëéèöóòûùçœey¥$£ß

sco clans

«Scottish Clan Names»
using the BD Jura font

«BD Jura»
Typedifferent font

2001

www.typedifferent.com

BD:217

northern clans

mackenzie
macrae
ross
mackay
gunn
munro
sinclair
chisholm

island & westcoast clans

macdonald
macleod
maclean
macneil

lowland clans

graham
wallace
scott
bruce
douglas
armstrong
napier

central highland clans

cameron
murray
stewart
anderson
henderson
macgregor
cumming
robertson
macmillan
menzies
macnab
macintyre
macdougall

southern highland clans

macnaughton
buchanan
colquhoun
macfarlane
campbell
macarthur
graham

cairngorms & eastcoast clans

clanchattan
mackintosh
shaw
macpherson
davidson
macgillivray
macbean
fraser
rose
broide
forbes
gordon
grant
mcduff

«BD GYMNASTICS»
1000x1000mm

2003

Unpublished

BD:218

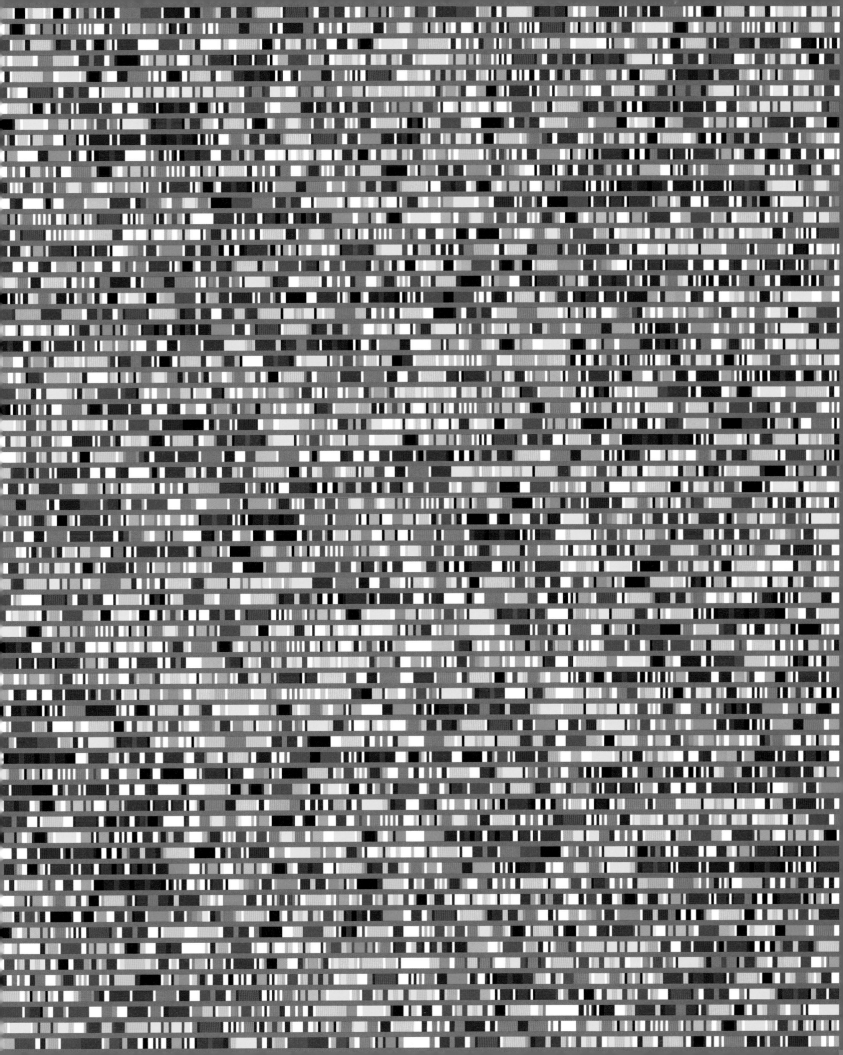

helvetica
lifestyle

«Helvetica Lifestyle»
Proposal for typographic
furniture

2002

Unpublished

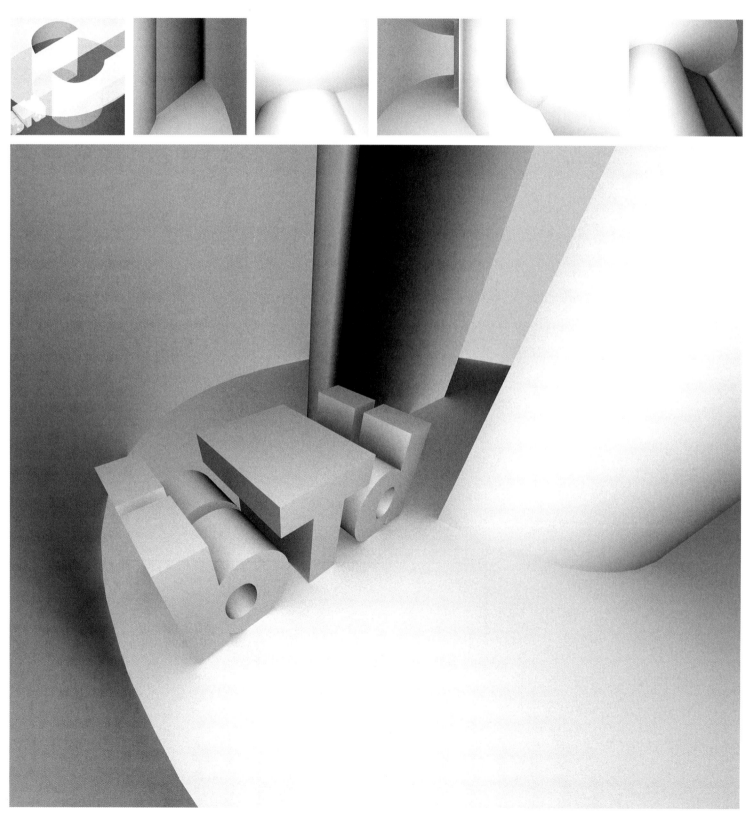

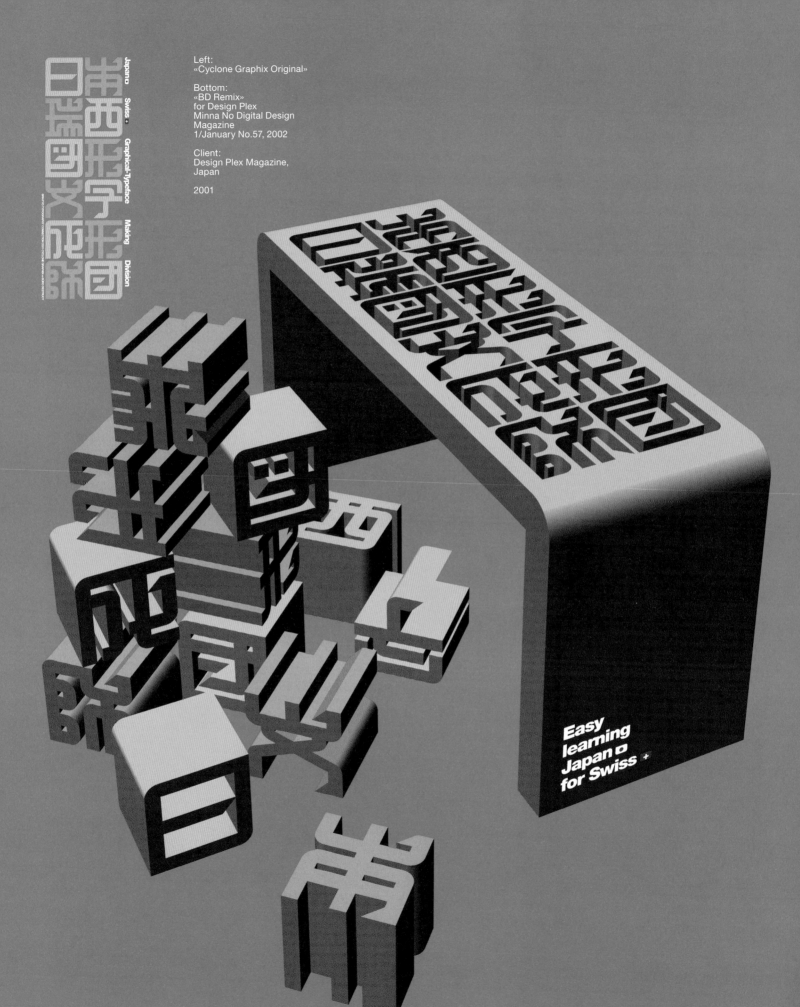

Left:
«Cyclone Graphix Original»

Bottom:
«BD Remix»
for Design Plex
Minna No Digital Design
Magazine
1/January No.57, 2002

Client:
Design Plex Magazine,
Japan

2001

Easy
learning
Japan
for Swiss +

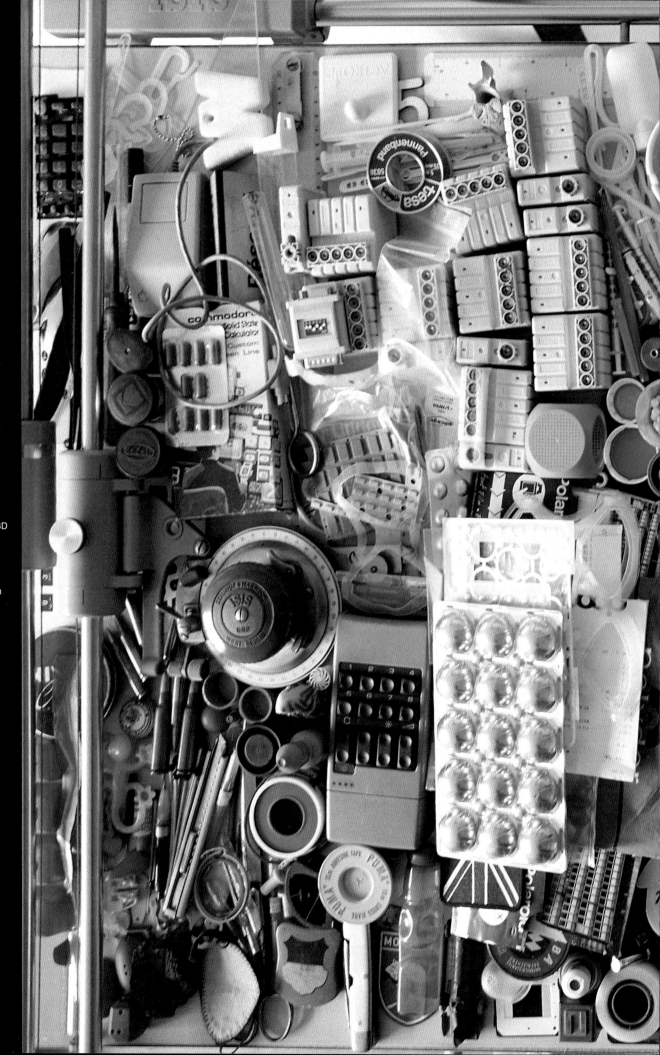

Lost items:

Lopetz:
Ricoh R1 photocamera
Ricoh RDC7 digitalcamera
Sharp ZQ-5650M organizer
400.– Swiss Francs
Deadend club membercard
DJ Shadow Entroducing CD
The Orb Toxygene Single CD
Towel and bathing suit

H1reber:
Bicycle
British navy beany
Sunglasses
1st Swatch
Bunch of keys
Laserpointer
1st Zippo
3 Zip's
15 Opticals
Dub backup three
Tricky, Maxinquaye CD
Leftfield, Leftism CD
FSUK 3 CD
Recloose, Cardiology CD

MBrunner:
Sunglasses
100.– Swiss Francs
2 Bicycles
Amulet
Ring
Bunch of keys
Gloves
Cap
Pair of shoes

Heiwid:
Nokia Mobile 8310
Nokia Mobile 6510
USB MP3 Pendrive
2 keys
350.– Swiss Francs

Moritz:
Nikon F5
Nikon flash SB28
Nikon lenses AF 35-70mm f/2.8D
Nikon lenses 50mm f/1.2
Nikon lenses 28mm f/2.8
Sony mobilephone Z5
Pulp Surfing CD
1 Snowbord glove
2 Mountainbikes
2 Yamaha scooter Neo's 50ccm
2 Arnette sunglasses

MADE IN TAIWAN

Adrian Etter • Adrian Frutiger • Adrian Peter • Adrian Scheidegger • Adrienne Leong • Afrika Bambaataa • Agustus Pablo • Air • Aki Kaurismäki • Akira • Al Hansen • Alina • Alphonse Mucha • Amelie • Amy Franceschini • Andreas Gursky • Andy Hug • Andy Warhol • Ane Hebeisen • Angela Pestalozzi • Anja Wiegmann • Antonio Sant'Elia • Aphex Twin • Apple Macintosh • Arling & Cameron • Art of Noise • Arthur Rimbaud • Aspirin • Ata Bozaci • Atom Heart • Auguste Piccard • Aurelio D. Spenato • Auron • Aya Christen • Balduin • Bandai • Banksy • Barry Weeden • Bauhaus • Beasty Boys • Beck • Benjamin Güdel • Benjamin Hirt • Bernadette Walter • Berner Ensemble • Bernhard Russi • Björk • Bill Sienkiewicz • Bio De Schaneiro • Boards of Canada • Bob Marley • Boba Fett • Boumi B • Brasserie Lorraine • Bret Easton Ellis • Brian Eno • Bruce Lee • Bruna Lüthi • Bungalow Records • Cabaret Voltaire • Cafe Kairo • Cafino • Candice Breitz • Capcom • Caro et Jeunet • Caro Hirt • Caroline Schreiber • Caspar Martig • Cervando • Charles & Ray Eames • Charles Reimers & Crew • Charles Spencer Chaplin • Chrigu Kohli • Christine Blau • Christoph Ballmer • Christoph Balsiger • Claes Oldenburg • Claudine Allemann • Club 111 • Cluster • Cohen Brothers • Commodore Amiga • Computer Chaos Club • Cornel Windlin • Costa Vece • Croci&Dufresne • Dada • Damian Hirst • Dana Purcz • Daniel «Jules» Schüler • Daniel Ihly • Daniel Miller • Daniel Scheppler • Daniel Torres • Daniel Wihler • David Bowie • David Fincher • David Holmes • David Lynch • De: Bug • Dell • Deninz • Dennis Hopper • Depeche Mode • Der kleine Maulwurf • Design Plex • Devilrobots • Die Gestalten • Dj Emely • Dj Food • Dj Hyper • Dj Krush • Dr. Norton • Dreamcast • Druckerei Brunner • Dustbowl • Echo • Edward D. Wood Jr. • Edward Norton • Egon Schiele • Elektrolux • Elio Pellin • Elvis Presley • Enki Bilal • Ethan Hawke • Eva Ursprung • F.S.O.L. • Fabian Wicki • Fat Boy Slim • Fat Gadget • Fee Liechti • Félix Nadar • Ferdinand Hodler • Fila Brazillia • Fischli & Weiss • Floria Sigismondi • Florian Wupperfeld • Francis Bacon • Francis Ford Coppola • Francis Foss • François Chalet • Frank Loyd Wright • Franz Gertsch • Fränzi Zuppinger • Fred • Freddy Fresh • Fri-Son • Fritz Haller • Fritz Kobi • Fritz Lang • Front 242 • Furifuri • Futura 2000 • G4 • Gabriel Le Mar • Gabriela «Doris» Kammermann • Gary Larson • Gary Oldman • Gasbook • George Clinton • Glen Robinson • Google • Grandmaster Flash • Greg Chapuisat • Gregor Wildermann • Gregory Gilbert-Lodge • Gruntz • G-Stone • Günther Netzer • Gustav Klimt • Guy Froidevaux • Guy Lafranchi • H.G. Wells • H.R. Giger • Hans-Rudolf Lutz • Harald Schmidt • Harald Szeemann • Hayao Miyazaki • Heidelberg • Heinz Edelmann • Heinz Hersberger • Helge Schneider • Helmut Newton • Helvetica Neue • Hendrik «Gytz» Thorsager • Herbie Hancock • Hergé • Hess is More • HGB Fideljus • Hideki Inaba • Hideo Kojima • Hi-Lite • Hooger Booger • Hope • Howard Jones • Hugo Wetli • Hydrogen Dukebox • Idea Magazine • IdN Sklam • Improware • Interdiscount • Invader • Iris Ruprecht • Itzli • J.C Hewlett • Jachie Mittoo • Jack Burton • Jaguar • Jan Rikus Hillmann • Jan T. Mazel • Jan Tuemer Berger • Jan Tümer • Jan Zuppinger • Jaqueline «Geisha» Wehrle • Jaques Tati • Jaques Uldry • Jaro Gielens • Jean Réno • Jean Seberg • Jean Ziegler • Jean-Michel Basquiat • Jeannie Casey • Jeff Mills • Jim Avignon • Jim Whiting • Jimi Hendrix • Jimi Tenor • Joel Peter Witkin • Johannes Gutenberg • John Carpender • John Lydon • Joost Swarte • Josef Müller-Brockmann • J-P Gaude • J-P Gaultier • Jules Verne • Junichi «Sav-Wo» Kitajima • Junko Tozaki • Jürg & Monique Küenzi • Jürg Lützelschwab • Kadiji • Kaleidophone • Karl Koch • Kaspar Lüthi • Kathi Jachmann • Keepy • Kemistry & Storm • Kenichiro Ueki • Kentaro «Ani» Fujimoto • Kevin Mueller • King Tubby • KLF • Konami • Kraftwerk • Kristen Wüthrich • Kulturhallen Dampfzentrale • Kurt Felix • Kurt Wirth • Kylie • Lang & Baumann • Lars Kordetzky • Laurence Desarzens • Laurin Merz • Le Corbusier • Le Sirupier de Berne • Lebbeus Woods • Leftfield • Leila Benaissa • Lia B. • Lila Prats • Lilo • Lorilleux International • Luke Vibert • Lulu • Luzi de Beaufort • Mac Winfield • Mad Max • Mahatma Ghandi • MalcolmX • Man Ray • Maniackers Design • Marc Ridet • Marcel Duchamp • Marco Mesot • Marco Reppeto • Marianne Weibel • Marion Meyer • Mark Pistel • Markus Reichenbach • Martin Lötscher • Masahiko Yendo • Massive Attack • Mattenpleger • Matthew Barney • Matthias Jost • Max Bill • Max Headroom • Max Henschel • Max Miedinger • Maxell • Mayumi Kaneko • MC 900ft Jesus • Meat Beat Manifesto • Mental Groove • Meret Oppenheim • Messer Chups • Metz & Nicole • Michael Bähni • Michael Gianfreda • Michael Meienberg • Michael Pfister • Michael Vögeli • Michel Houellebecq • Mie Owashi • Migros • Mike Eskimo • Mike Skinner • Milla Jovovich • Mina «Sevgi» Tuemer Berger • Mirco Brunner • Mo Wax • Moloko • Monteverdi • Moulin Rouge • Nadine Borter • Namco • Natascha Sturny • Natsume • Neil Armstrong • Nelson Mandela • Nendo Graphics • Neotropic • Neville Brody • New Order • Newtek • Nicole Beutler • Nightmares on Wax • Ninja Tune • Nintendo • Noëmi Droux • Norm • Nova Huta • Nudle • Nyce • Oddworld Inhabitants • ÖffÖff • Olaf Breuning • Oliver Bondzio • Oliver Hofer • Olmo • ORB • Orbital • Oscar Niemeyer • Ovomaltine • Pac Man • Paco Suarez • Page • Parisienne • PatG & Sascha • Paul Klee • Paul Rand • Pedä Siegrist • Pele • Peter Bichsel • Peter Blake • Peter Greenaway • Peter Jackson • Peter Zemp • Philip K. Dick • Philippe Hansen • Philippe Parreno • Pia Affolter • Pier Paolo Pasolini • Pink Floyd • Pius Freiburghaus • Plaid • Playstation • Plump DJ's • Polaroid • Pork • Postscript • Power Graphixx • Priska Krebs • Pro Helvetia • Prodigy • Promacx • Promptcomputer • Quentin Tarantino • Ramax • Raffinerie • Raoul Cannemeijer • Raymond Loewy • Regula Roost • Reid Miles • Reitschule Bern • Remo Stoller • René Magrit • Renegade Soundwave • Renzo Piano • Richard Hell • Ridley Scott • Rikku • Robby Naish • Robert & Sybille Riesen • Robert Anton Wilson • Robert Wagner • Robin Hood • Roland • Roland Mueller • Roman Signer • Ronald Steckel • Rooibos Tea • Rosmarie • Röyksopp • Rudi Gernreich • Ryota «Vectorscan» • Ryuko Kazutomo • Saab • Sabine Adler • Sabine Eva Wittwer • Sandra Moser • Sandro • Santiago Calatrava • Santorini • Sarah Lauper • Scritti Politti • Severed Heads • Severin Aegerter • SfGB • Shawn Palmer • Shift Japan • Shin Sasaki • Siegfried Brunner • Simeon Reusser • Simon Fehlmann • Simon Schweingruber • Sims • Sir Henry Segrave • Skint • Soccer Team Wabern • soDA • Sofie's • Solid Snake • Sonja • Sony • Sophie Taeuber Arp • Squarepusher • Squaresoft • Stanley Kubrick • Stefan «SWo» Wolf • Stefan Ingold • Stefan Riesen • Stefanie Ledermann • Stelarc • Stephen Hawking • Stereo MCs • Stranglers • Studs Terkel • Sue Liechti • Supermario • Swifty • Syd Mead • T.C. Boyle • Taito • Takashi Murakami • Talk Talk • TDK • Team Ultraviolet • Technics • Tekjam • Terry Gilliam • The Beatles • The Clash • The Designers Republic • The Easy Alohas • The Face • The Professionals • The Young Gods • Thomas Alva Edison • Thomas Demand • Thomson Twins • Timothy Leary • Todd Levin • Tom Aellen • Tom Ellard • Tomato • Tsuyoshi Kusano • Ugo Rondinone • Uma Thurman • Urs Althaus • Urs Bänninger • Urs Mühlemann • Urs Wenger • Urs Widmer • Urs Zaugg • Ursula Merki • Uwe Wittwer • Valentina Tereschkowa • Van Gogh TV • Varicolor • Velokurier • Verner Panton • Versiontracker • Vilém Flusser • Vivi • Wagon Christ • Wale Buri • Wally Badarou • Walter Van Beirendonck • Walther Gropius • Warp • Wei Long • Weltschmertz • Werner • Willhelm Tell • William Gibson • Xerox • Yoshinori Sunhara • Yoshitomo Nara • Yuka Takeda • Yukiko «Yan» Yano • Yuko Christen • Zaha Hadid • Zera Huber • and our Families